BELIEVING IN
NARNIA

A Kid's Guide to

UNLOCKING SECRET SYMBOLS OF FAITH

in C. S. Lewis's

The Chronicles of Narnia

NATALIE
GILLESPIE

THOMAS NELSON
Since 1798

NASHVILLE   DALLAS   MEXICO CITY   RIO DE JANEIRO   BEIJING

BELIEVING IN NARNIA: A KID'S GUIDE TO UNLOCKING SECRET SYMBOLS OF FAITH IN C. S. LEWIS'S THE CHRONICLES OF NARNIA
© 2008 by Natalie Nichols Gillespie

Published in Nashville, Tennessee, by Thomas Nelson. Thomas Nelson is a registered trademark of Thomas Nelson, Inc.

Thomas Nelson, Inc., titles may be purchased in bulk for educational, business, fund-raising, or sales promotional use. For information, please e-mail SpecialMarkets@ThomasNelson.com.

This book is the author's interpretation of and commentary on The Chronicles of Narnia. It was not written by, in consultation with, or endorsed by the author, the estate of C. S. Lewis, or the publisher of The Chronicles of Narnia, nor is it a part of the series The Chronicles of Narnia.

THE CHRONICLES OF NARNIA by C. S. Lewis copyright © C. S. Lewis Pte. Ltd. 1950, 1951, 1952, 1953, 1954, 1955, 1956. Extracts reprinted by permission.

All Scripture quotations are taken from the INTERNATIONAL CHILDREN'S BIBLE®. © 1986, 1988, 1999 by Thomas Nelson, Inc. All rights reserved.

Page design by: Mandi Cofer
Illustrations by: Kay Meadows
Doodles by: Casey Hooper, Lori Lynch, and Walter Petrie

Library of Congress Cataloging-in-Publication Data

Gillespie, Natalie Nichols.
    Believing in Narnia : a kid's guide to unlocking the secret symbols of faith in C. S. Lewis's The chronicles of Narnia / Natalie Nichols Gillespie.
      p. cm.
    ISBN 978-1-4003-1282-5 (softcover)
    1. Lewis, C. S. (Clive Staples), 1898-1963. Chronicles of Narnia—Juvenile literature. 2. Children—Books and reading—Great Britain—History—20th century—Juvenile literature. 3. Children's stories, English—History and criticism—Juvenile literature. 4. Christian fiction, English—History and criticism—Juvenile literature. 5. Fantasy fiction, English—History and criticism—Juvenile literature. 6. Narnia (Imaginary place)—Juvenile literature. I. Title.
PR6023.E926C5334 2008
823'.912—dc22

2007052530

Printed in the United States of America
08 09 10 11 12 RRD 9 8 7 6 5 4 3 2 1

The interior paper is made from 100% recycled fiber.

To my brave Narnia fans,

Joshua and Justin

May you always seek to get closer
to the real Aslan, Jesus Christ,
and continue to grow "further up, further in."

CONTENTS

Contents

THIS BOOK IS FOR BRAVE KIDS ONLY!

If you are holding this book in your hands, you're holding a key that will unlock some of the secrets to another world—the world of Narnia.

The Chronicles of Narnia are fantasy books written by the famous author C. S. Lewis. They are some of the best-selling and most-loved books of all time, with about one hundred million copies sold. While these stories aren't true, the secrets you will uncover in them are real, and—psst, I'll let you in on a secret right now—they can help you  THAT'S A LOT OF BOOKS! learn more about Jesus and see Him more clearly. Isn't that cool?

When Lucy falls through the wardrobe in *The Lion, the Witch and the Wardrobe* and enters the land of Narnia, it is like she discovers a land of treasure, filled with secrets and symbols and things she'd never seen. She has to be brave to face the strange, new world she finds there.

In the book *Prince Caspian*, the prince has to run for his life from his mean uncle. "Dear Prince, you must leave this castle at once and go to seek your fortune in the wide world. Your life is in danger here," his teacher tells him.

Many characters in the Chronicles have to be brave, and now it's your turn. You get to be brave like Lucy and Caspian as you read this book. You'll need the courage to dig deeper, explore, and go beyond the surface to uncover the secrets that lie underneath the stories of Narnia.

Narnia is a world of talking animals, magical potions, and bloody battles. It's a fantastical place filled with Fauns and Centaurs, an all-powerful lion, an evil queen, a mighty mouse, and children who become kings and queens. Check this out: Narnia is also full of secrets, symbols, and hidden clues that tell stories *inside* the stories.

There are a lot of books about Narnia, but this is one written just for you.

It isn't a picture book for little kids, and it wasn't written for your parents. It was written for you, with Narnia facts and questions from kids like you. (Look for places that say "Justin Time" and "Joshua's Journey" to see what real kids learned and asked about Narnia's secrets.)

So if you're prepared to travel to other worlds, bravely face the unexpected, and dive deeply into the mysteries under the surface of the stories, let's go to Narnia to unlock the secret symbols of faith in the Chronicles.

Unlocking the Secrets for Reading This Book

The first thing you need to know about this book is that it is full of twists, turns, and surprises—a lot like the adventures in Narnia. C. S. Lewis actually talks about Jesus a lot in these seven books. You just have to know where to look to find Him. Hopefully, by the end of this book you will know that believing in Narnia means believing in Jesus, the Savior of the whole world. The hope and joy He will bring to your life is like the hope and joy He brought to the characters in these seven books.

The Chronicles of Narnia are full of secrets that point to Jesus and the Bible. Sometimes the secret is in a name; sometimes it is in what a character says or how he or she acts. Sometimes it is in the way C. S. Lewis describes Aslan. After you read this book, you will be able to experience

The Chronicles of Narnia again (or for the very first time) and see some of these hidden symbols. It's kind of like putting on the special glasses that help you see a 3-D movie. Before you put on the glasses, the movie screen looks flat and the images are fuzzy. After you put on the glasses, the action on the screen jumps out at you.

Before you get started, you'll need to recognize some symbols for the journey.

When you see one of these symbols, it means that this is a quote from one of The Chronicles of Narnia. Sometimes a quote is followed by the abbreviation of the book so you can hunt for it yourself. The abbreviations and symbols used in this book look like this:

 *The Magician's Nephew (MN)*

 The Lion, the Witch and the Wardrobe (LWW)

 The Horse and His Boy (HHB)

Prince Caspian (PC)

The Voyage of the Dawn Treader (VDT)

The Silver Chair (SC)

The Last Battle (LB)

When you see this symbol, it's like discovering treasure, because you have found one of the secret places where C. S. Lewis hints at something you can find in the Bible. The Bible verse will be marked with this symbol.

When you see this page, you are entering a secret door where you will learn one of Narnia's Greatest Secrets, just like the characters in the Chronicles did. These are real-life lessons that Aslan taught and that God wants you to learn too.

Each section of this book is a "key" to unlocking some of the most important secrets in the Chronicles. The first one will help you if you have never read The Chronicles of Narnia or need to refresh your memory. The first key includes a short summary of each of the seven books so you'll know what's going on. The next keys will help you discover how some of the people, places, and things in Narnia hold secrets about real-life faith, and you can uncover the secrets of your own faith by answering the questions you find at the end of each part.

Finally, you can also unlock secrets in the life of the author, C. S. Lewis, and find other books and Web sites to learn more about Narnia in the last keys at the end of this book.

So, brave seekers, now that you know how to unlock the doors to the mysteries of Narnia, go to the next section and get ready to turn the second key . . .

definitely a cool dude

Unlocking the Stories of The Chronicles of Narnia

The Chronicles of Narnia can be read in any order, but if you want to read them in the order of the Narnian time in which they happened, you would read *The Magician's Nephew* first, because it tells how Narnia was created by Aslan and how evil entered Narnia. Next, you would read *The Lion, the Witch and the Wardrobe*, which tells how the Pevensie children became the kings and queens of Narnia. It takes place a thousand Narnia years after the creation of Narnia. *The Horse and His Boy* takes place during the reign of Peter, Susan, Edmund, and Lucy; and *Prince Caspian* begins hundreds of Narnia years later, when Cair Paravel lies in ruins and Caspian must defeat his bad Uncle Miraz. *The Voyage of the Dawn*

Narnia time is different than our time

Treader is three Narnia years after that, followed by *The Silver Chair*, about three hundred and fifty Narnia years later. Finally, *The Last Battle* and the end of Narnia takes place about two hundred years after Eustace, Jill, and Puddleglum rescue Prince Rilian.

This is not the order C. S. Lewis wrote or published the Chronicles, but it is the order he suggested people read them, so that's the order they are listed here. Here is a brief retelling of what happens in each book, but for the most fun you'll want to read each book for yourself.

The Magician's Nephew

The Magician's Nephew was the sixth book published, but it is really the first story about Narnia. In this story, the land of Narnia is created by Aslan the Lion. The book begins in London when a boy named Digory Kirke and a girl named Polly Plummer become next-door neighbors and friends. Digory's mother is very ill, and he and his mom are staying with his strange Uncle Andrew Ketterley.

One day the kids accidentally end up in Uncle Andrew's room in the attic. Uncle Andrew gives Polly a magic yellow ring, and she disappears and can't get back. Digory follows Polly, and they find themselves in the Wood between the Worlds. After some arguing, they decide to take the magic rings and jump into a pool of water to see if it leads to yet another world. They find a deserted castle and a banquet hall with hundreds of people who are under a spell. Digory rings a magic bell, and the evil Queen Jadis of Charn comes to life.

Jadis (also known as the Witch) grabs the children and wants to be taken back to Digory and Polly's world. Digory and Polly are horrified and quickly stick their hands in their pockets to touch the rings so they will go back to the Wood between the Worlds. Unfortunately, the Witch grabs Polly's hair and gets pulled into the wood too. The kids then put the other rings on to go back to London, but Jadis grabs Digory's ear and ends up in London with them.

there's a 316-foot-tall clock tower named Big Ben in London

In London, the Witch makes a lot of trouble, and the police start chasing her. Digory and Polly grab the Witch, touch a magic ring, and end up back in the Wood between the Worlds, but along with the Witch come the cabby, the horse, and Uncle Andrew! Polly and Digory jump into another pool with everyone and end up in a world of nothing.

Then they hear singing, and stars appear. Aslan creates the entire land of Narnia and all its creatures through his song. He makes the cabby and his wife the first king and queen of Narnia. Aslan declares some of the animals and trees to be talking beasts. Digory asks Aslan to help his sick mother, and Aslan sends him to get a seed from an apple in a faraway land, so it will grow into a tree in Narnia that will keep the Witch away.

Digory and Polly ride on a winged horse to get the seed. They find a gated garden, and Digory goes in to get the apple. He is tempted to eat one of the shining silvery apples, but he doesn't. He sees the Witch eating one, and she tempts Digory to eat one, but again he doesn't. He takes the apple to Aslan, and it becomes the tree that protects Narnia. The next day Aslan gives Digory an apple from the newly grown tree and tells him to take it home to heal his mother. Digory, Polly, and Uncle Andrew go back to England.

Digory's mother is healed by the apple, and Digory throws the core in the garden. Digory and Polly plant the magic rings in a circle around the apple core. Digory moves to a huge house in the country and grows up to be a professor. He makes the old apple tree into a wardrobe, the same wardrobe that the Pevensie children go through to find Narnia.

The Lion, the Witch and the Wardrobe

The Lion, the Witch and the Wardrobe is the first book C. S. Lewis wrote about Narnia, and it is the story of the Pevensie children—Peter, Susan, Edmund, and Lucy. These brothers and sisters are sent from London to a professor's house in the country to be safe during World War II. The Pevensies explore the big house and find a wardrobe that Lucy climbs into and finds herself in another world called Narnia.

WORLD WAR II HAPPENED FROM 1939 to 1945

She meets a Faun named Mr. Tumnus and goes to his house for tea. Mr. Tumnus tells Lucy that he is supposed to turn her over to the White Witch, who has cast a spell over Narnia so that it is always winter but never Christmas. Mr. Tumnus lets Lucy go instead, and she reenters the wardrobe.

Lucy's brothers and sister do not believe her about Narnia, and Edmund teases her. On the next rainy day, the siblings play hide-and-seek, and Edmund follows Lucy into the wardrobe and then into Narnia. The White Witch, Jadis, pulls up on her sledge and begins questioning Edmund. When she finds out he is a human, she pretends to be nice and magically gives him his favorite candy, Turkish Delight. The White Witch says she will make Edmund a king if he brings his brother and sisters to her.

When Lucy and Edmund return through the wardrobe, Edmund lies and says that Lucy is just pretending about Narnia. But a few days later, all four children find themselves in Narnia. They meet Mr. Beaver, who tells them that Aslan the Lion is coming. He also tells them that an ancient prophecy says four human children will bring an end to the White Witch's reign. The children do not know Aslan, but Peter, Susan, and Lucy feel in their hearts that he is the "good" side.

Mr. Beaver warns the children that the White Witch will try to kill them. Edmund, who thinks the White Witch is good, sneaks out of the Beavers' house and goes to the Witch's castle.

Mr. and Mrs. Beaver, Peter, Susan, and Lucy run to find Aslan before the Witch gets them. They hide in a cave as the winter spell starts to break, and Father Christmas visits them and gives them gifts. In the meantime, Edmund makes it to the Witch's castle and discovers that she has turned many creatures into statues. The Witch makes Edmund her prisoner and takes him with her to try to catch Peter, Susan, and Lucy.

Peter, Susan, Lucy, and the Beavers find Aslan and tell him about Edmund's betrayal. The White Witch is about to kill Edmund when some of Narnia's good animals stop her. They save Edmund, but the Witch escapes. Edmund meets Aslan, and they talk. Edmund apologizes to his brother and sisters and is changed from then on.

The Witch meets with Aslan and reminds him that traitors to Narnia must be killed or all of Narnia will be destroyed. Aslan offers to take Edmund's punishment, and the White Witch and her followers tie Aslan to the Stone Table and kill him as Lucy and Susan watch. The White Witch's army then heads off to fight Aslan's followers.

Just as it looks like there is no hope, Aslan comes to life again and takes Susan and Lucy to the battle where their brothers are fighting the Witch and her followers. Peter is fighting the Witch, and Aslan kills her. When Edmund is wounded, Lucy uses a healing potion to help him and the others who are hurt. The Witch's side is defeated, and Aslan, the Pevensie children, and the good creatures head to the castle called Cair Paravel. The children become the Kings and Queens of Narnia, and Aslan leaves.

Lion groups are called prides.
Aslan traveled alone.

Peter, Susan, Edmund, and Lucy reign in Narnia for a long time and forget about their other life in England. Many Narnia years later, they go off to hunt the White Stag and find the lamp-post in the forest. It seems familiar to them, and they find themselves in the wardrobe again, discovering that no time on earth has passed since they left.

The Horse and His Boy

The Horse and His Boy takes place when Peter, Susan, Edmund, and Lucy were the Kings and Queens of Narnia. Far south in the land of Calormen, where a king called the Tisroc rules, a fisherman named Arsheesh lives with his boy named Shasta. One day an important-looking stranger called a Tarkaan comes from the South and has dinner at Shasta's house. The man wants to buy Shasta to be his slave, and Shasta overhears Arsheesh bargaining with the man. He also hears Arsheesh tell the man that Shasta is not really his son, that he found him in a little boat that washed ashore when Shasta was a baby.

When Shasta hears this, he is relieved because Arsheesh often beat him, and he doesn't love him like a son should love his father. Shasta decides to run away rather than be sold to the Tarkaan. He walks over to the Tarkaan's horse, and it begins to talk! It tells him that it has been kidnapped from Narnia, and that the Tarkaan is very cruel. Shasta and the Talking Horse, Bree, begin to head toward Narnia.

Shasta and Bree travel north along the coast for weeks and weeks. One cloudy night, they hear a horse and rider near them. They discover that the other horse is also a Talking Horse named Hwin and her rider is a Tarkeena named Aravis. They are also trying to escape to Narnia, and the four decide to go together.

Aravis tells the others that she is the descendant of a great Tisroc, and her father and stepmother have promised her in marriage to a cruel, old man. Rather than marry him, she decided to kill herself. But just as she was about to plunge a dagger into her heart, Hwin talked to her for the first time and stopped her. The two of them made a plan to run away to Narnia, where both could be free.

The four travel together to the city of Tashbaan. They disguise themselves and begin walking through the city. Shasta is grabbed by a procession of Narnians who mistake him for the runaway son of King Lune of Archenland. King Edmund takes Shasta to a room where Queen Susan of Narnia calls him "Corin" and tells him he is naughty for running away. Shasta goes along with them because he is afraid to tell them the truth. Later that day, the real Prince Corin (the son of King Lune of Archenland) climbs in the window. The boys talk for a few minutes, and Shasta goes out the window to meet Bree, Hwin, and Aravis.

It turns out that King Edmund and Queen Susan were visiting Tashbaan because the Tisroc's son, Rabadash, wants to marry Queen Susan. Susan decides Rabadash is a bad man, and the Narnians escape in the night on their ship.

Meanwhile, Aravis runs into a friend, Lasaraleen, who recognizes her and takes her to the palace and hides her. Aravis and Lasaraleen overhear the Tisroc and Prince Rabadash plotting against Narnia because Susan has escaped. Rabadash plans to overtake Archenland and get to Narnia before the ship arrives. Then he will grab Susan as soon as they set foot on shore.

Aravis sneaks away from the palace, and she and Shasta and the horses set off to warn King Lune that Rabadash is on his way. They come to a Hermit's house, and he sends Shasta on alone. Shasta warns King Lune, then gets lost and ends up in Narnia, where he encounters Aslan and realizes that Aslan has always been taking care of him.

Queen Susan, Archenland, and Narnia are saved, and they defeat the Calormenes led by Prince Rabadash, who is turned into a donkey by Aslan when he will not repent. Shasta finds out he is really Cor, King Lune's son and Corin's twin, who was kidnapped. _That's why they look alike!_ Shasta and Aravis eventually get married and have a son named Ram the Great, the most famous king of Archenland.

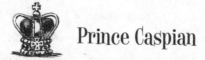# Prince Caspian

Prince Caspian occurs one London year after Peter, Susan, Edmund, and Lucy went to Narnia through the wardrobe, and the children are waiting on a train platform to go back to school. Suddenly they feel like they are being pulled and find themselves standing in some woods.

They discover it is the grounds of Cair Paravel, their old castle. It has been hundreds of years in Narnia time, and Cair Paravel is in ruins. Still, they find their old castle filled with treasure and the gifts they received from Father Christmas in *The Lion, the Witch and the Wardrobe.*

The Pevensies spend the night on the ground, and the next morning they see a boat coming near the shore and two men throw a struggling bundle into the water. Susan shoots an arrow at one of the men, and they swim away. The Pevensies rescue the bundle and find a Dwarf. He tells them that he is a messenger of King Caspian, the Telmarine who is now King of Narnia, and he tells them Caspian's story.

Caspian had been raised by his uncle, King Miraz, and aunt, Queen Prunaprismia, because his parents were dead. Caspian's nurse tells him stories of Old Narnia, when animals could talk and Aslan made appearances. King Miraz gets angry when Caspian shares the stories with him, and he sends Caspian's nurse away and gets him a tutor named Doctor Cornelius. It turns out that Doctor Cornelius is part Dwarf (an Old Narnian) and secretly continues teaching Caspian about Old Narnia.

After a few years, Queen Prunaprismia has a baby boy. Doctor Cornelius tells Caspian that King Miraz killed Caspian's father and took the throne from Caspian, who was the rightful heir. Now he will want his own son to be king, and Caspian must run away. Doctor Cornelius gives Caspian an ivory horn (Susan's magical horn) and tells him to blow it only when he is in the greatest danger.

Caspian leaves, hits his head on a branch, and gets caught by a badger and two Dwarfs who are Old Narnians. Trufflehunter, Trumpkin, and Nikabrik take Caspian to meet all the Old Narnians who are in hiding. He meets bears, squirrels, more Dwarfs, and Centaurs, who all welcome Caspian as the true king. They form a war council, including a mouse named Reepicheep.

The war council decides to go to Aslan's How, the ancient hill of the Stone Table, to go to war. Miraz's army and Caspian's army fight for days, and Miraz's army is stronger than they expected. Caspian and his council decide to blow Susan's horn, and they send messengers to Cair Paravel's ruins and to Lantern Waste (where the lamp-post is) to see if help will arrive. Trumpkin the Dwarf goes to Cair Paravel and is captured. He is dumped in the water and then rescued by the Pevensie children.

Peter, Susan, Edmund, and Lucy go with Trumpkin to Aslan's How. Aslan appears to Lucy to show them the way, but the others don't believe her because they can't see him, and they head into a dangerous situation. That night Aslan tells Lucy she should have followed him no matter what anyone else decided. She wakes everyone and tells them they must follow Aslan. Although they don't all believe, they do follow her.

Finally, they can all see Aslan, and Edmund and Peter arrive at Aslan's How. Peter sends a challenge to King Miraz to fight him man-to-man, and he accepts. Peter beats Miraz, the trees and mythical creatures of Old Narnia join the battle, and the Telmarines are defeated. Caspian is crowned, and a great celebration follows.

have you ever seen a tree fight?

Aslan offers all Telmarines the chance to stay in Narnia or to go back to the earth, which is where they were originally from. Some stay, and some go through a doorway that Aslan creates. The Pevensies also go through the doorway and find themselves back at the train platform, as though no time has passed at all.

The Voyage of
the Dawn Treader

In *The Voyage of the Dawn Treader*, Edmund and Lucy Pevensie are sent to spend the summer with their cousin Eustace Clarence Scrubb, a very unpleasant boy. Edmund and Lucy are looking at a picture on the wall of a Narnian ship, when Eustace comes in and teases them about their "make-believe" country.

Eustace tries to grab the picture off the wall, and all three end up in the sea, where King Caspian dives in and saves them. Caspian tells Edmund and Lucy it's been three Narnia years since he became king, and he is on a mission to find seven friends of his father who were sent away by his cruel Uncle Miraz. Reepicheep is with him and hopes they will reach the end of the world and find Aslan's Country. Eustace just complains.

The *Dawn Treader* then voyages past the Lone Islands. On the island of Felimath, Caspian, Lucy, Edmund, Eustace, and Reepicheep are captured by slave traders. Lord Bern, one of the seven men Caspian is looking for, buys Caspian. Caspian reveals his identity, and Caspian kicks the bad Governor Gumpas out of office and makes Bern the Duke of the Lone Islands. Caspian frees all the slaves, including Lucy, Eustace, and Reepicheep, and they set sail again toward the east.

They escape a storm and a sea serpent and find several islands. On one of the islands, they find one Narnian lord who is dead, and Eustace is turned into a dragon. Later his dragon skin is peeled away by Aslan, and Eustace begins to change into a nicer boy after that. On another island they find another dead lord, and they name this island Deathwater Island, for it has a pool of water that turns everything into gold (and they almost step in it!).

Next, they come to an island inhabited by a magician who used to be

a star. The magician takes care of some silly, invisible creatures called
Dufflepuds, who want Lucy to read the magician's book and undo the
spell that makes them invisible. Lucy reads the book and is tempted to
try a couple of spells for herself, but Aslan's face appears in the book and
scares her from doing it. Lucy finds the spell to make things visible and
says it—and Aslan appears. He introduces her to the magician, and the
Dufflepuds remain silly.

Next, the ship sails into a pitch-black cloud, where all dreams (even
CREEPY nightmares) come true. They rescue Lord Rhoop, one
of the seven men, but get stuck in the darkness and
start hearing things from their bad dreams. Lucy cries out to Aslan, and
a big bird called an albatross (that is really Aslan) brings them out of the
darkness.

They sail on and find an island with a table set with a great feast. The
remaining three lords are at the end of the table in an enchanted sleep. A
beautiful girl appears, and Caspian asks her how to wake the sleepers.
The girl says he must meet her father. Ramandu appears, and the girl and
Ramandu (who was once a star) sing and seem to make the sun rise. The
old man tells Caspian that to break the spell they must sail to the world's
end and leave someone there.

As the ship sails on, they find water that is sweet, like drinkable light,
and then see lilies everywhere. They land, and Reepicheep plans to leave
and head for the end of the world to find Aslan's Country. Caspian wants
to go with him but must return since he is the king. Aslan meets them and
tells Caspian that Eustace, Edmund, and Lucy will go with Reepicheep.
Reepicheep goes to the mountains, never to be seen again. Caspian marries Ramandu's daughter, and they sail back to Narnia.

The kids get out on a huge, grassy plain and find a lamb that asks
them to eat. The lamb becomes Aslan, who tells them they will not be
coming back to Narnia. Then he tears open the sky, and the children find
themselves back in the bedroom again.

The Silver Chair

One London year after the adventures on the *Dawn Treader*, Eustace Scrubb is at school and finds classmate Jill Pole crying because she is being bullied. He tells her about Narnia and decides they should ask Aslan to take them there. Eustace and Jill walk through a door that they think leads out of the schoolyard but actually takes them into another world. They are at the edge of a cliff when Jill tries to show off and gets too close. Eustace grabs for her and falls over, but Aslan appears and blows his breath in Eustace's direction, and Eustace is carried off to the west.

Jill meets Aslan and is very afraid. He tells her that she and Eustace are to save the lost Prince of Narnia, who disappeared ten years ago after his mother was killed in the woods by a serpent. Aslan gives Jill four signs and then blows her toward Narnia too. She lands near Cair Paravel, where she finds Eustace, and they see an old king setting sail on his ship. It is Caspian, and it has been seventy Narnia years since the voyage of the *Dawn Treader*. It is Caspian's son who is missing.

Jill and Eustace are taken by owls to the house of a Marsh-wiggle named Puddleglum, and he goes with them on their quest. They start walking, try-ing to find Aslan's signs. They meet a royal-looking lady with a knight who doesn't speak. She tells them to stop at the gentle giants' castle in Harfang for refreshment. Instead of sticking to Aslan's instructions, Eustace and Jill go to the giants' castle instead, and the giants plan to eat them.

They escape and end up underground in Underland, where gnomes live with the wicked Queen of Underland and a young human, who is under an enchantment. The Queen and the man are the same two people they met on the road, and the Queen was the one who told them to visit the giants. The young man tells them that the Queen is making the gnomes build underground tunnels below an earthly kingdom (which turns out to be Narnia), so that they can break through, destroy the kingdom, and live on earth as its rulers. The young man seems very pleased with the idea.

Next, the young man warns Eustace, Jill, and Puddleglum that he is under an enchantment, and each night he turns into a madman, then a horrible serpent. He is tied up at night by the gnomes so that he doesn't hurt anyone. Eustace, Jill, and Puddleglum decide to sneak in and watch him that night as he changes. What actually happens is that at night the spell breaks and he remembers that he is really Prince Rilian of Narnia, and he says Aslan's name. This is Aslan's sign, and Puddleglum and Eustace cut the bindings. They all start to leave when the Queen, who is actually a Witch, returns.

The Witch tries to enchant them by making them so sleepy that they forget about Narnia, but Puddleglum steps into the fire to wake himself up and reminds the others about Aslan. The Witch turns herself into a serpent, and Rilian kills her. Her spells are broken, and Underland begins to be destroyed by floods. The gnomes flee back to the center of the earth, where they were taken from.

The others find the place where the gnomes had been digging tunnels, dig their way out, and find themselves back in Narnia. There is great celebration, and the next morning King Caspian returns. He is very ill, speaks to Prince Rilian briefly, and then dies.

Aslan appears, and the children are taken back to his mountain, where they see King Caspian lying dead in a pool. Aslan tells Eustace to prick his paw with a thorn, and when Aslan's blood drops into the water, Caspian awakes and is young again. He will live forever in Aslan's Country, but Aslan sends Eustace and Jill back to London, with Caspian at their side for just a few minutes to scare off the bullies when they get a brief look at him.

The Last Battle

In *The Last Battle*, it has been hundreds of Narnia years since King Rilian took the throne. His descendant, King Tirian, is in his hunting lodge when he hears that Aslan has been seen again in Narnia.

What really is happening is that a tricky Talking Ape named Shift and his not-very-smart donkey friend Puzzle have found a lion skin. Shift dresses Puzzle in it to make everyone think Aslan is back so they will obey him.

King Tirian and his best friend, Jewel the Unicorn, are excited that Aslan is back, until a Dryad comes to them and reports that the Talking Trees are being cut down in Lantern Waste. Tirian and Jewel set out to see who is murdering the trees.

Near Lantern Waste, they see a water rat making a raft out of tree trunks. The rat tells them the trees are being murdered on Aslan's orders, and King Tirian and Jewel are horrified. When they see two Calormenes (warriors from a neighboring land) cutting down trees and beating a Talking Horse, they kill the two men.

Tirian realizes he has done a terrible thing by killing the two men, and he and Jewel turn themselves over to the Calormenes to be judged by Aslan. They are taken to Shift, who is keeping the Aslan-dressed Puzzle out of sight and answering all requests for Aslan. Shift tells all the animals that they are going to be sent to work for the Calormenes because Aslan has made a deal with their god, Tash. He then has King Tirian tied to a tree.

That night Tirian calls out to Aslan to come to Narnia or to send the children from the other world to help Narnia. Tirian sees a vision of a table with seven people around it who all look shocked to see him. The next morning two of those people come to Tirian and untie him. They are Eustace Scrubb and Jill Pole, who had been visiting Professor Digory Kirke, along with Polly Plummer, and Peter, Edmund, and Lucy Pevensie. The seven had gathered to talk about Narnia because the Professor had a feeling Narnia needed them. When they saw Tirian, they knew it was true.

Peter and Edmund go back to Digory's old house and dig up the magic rings so Eustace and Jill can get back to Narnia, but Aslan blows them with his breath to Narnia without the rings.

Tirian, Eustace, and Jill go to the stable and rescue Jewel and Puzzle, but Shift and the head of the Calormenes, along with Ginger, a traitorous leopard, continue to deceive the people and creatures of Narnia. King Tirian shows himself and tries to get the Narnians to believe that Aslan would never treat them this way, but many turn against him and Aslan.

A battle of the two sides breaks out, and Eustace, Jill, and Tirian are surrounded. During the battle, they each enter the stable and find themselves suddenly through a door to Aslan's Country. They find glorious fruit, meet Aslan, and are reunited with old friends. Then they watch as Aslan brings about the end of Old Narnia, bringing all the animals who believed in him through the door while the others turn away. At last, the sun is extinguished, water covers Narnia, and it is no more.

CAN YOU SAY "HEAVEN"?

Eustace, Jill, and Tirian discover that they are in a world where they will never get tired, never hurt, never fear, and never grow old. Aslan tells them that they have died, and now they have to go "further up, further in." As they do, they see that they are in a new Narnia, and that the further they go, the bigger and better each land gets. They are reunited with Peter, Edmund, and Lucy, as well as Caspian and others, and truly live happily ever after.

Unlocking the Secrets of Characters and Creatures

Some of the biggest secrets in The Chronicles of Narnia are locked inside the characters and creatures in the world C. S. Lewis created in these seven books. Each of the major characters like Peter, Edmund, and Lucy—plus Prince Caspian, King Tirian, Shasta, Eustace, Jill, and others—grow in their faith as they face their fears and faults and come face-to-face with the mighty lion, Aslan. They learn to trust him, and they fight great fights to make sure that good wins over evil.

As you turn the third key and unlock the secrets of the characters and creatures in the Chronicles, you will discover truths that will help you grow in your own faith in Jesus.

Secret Signs
in the
Good Characters

Aslan the Lion

➤ (The only character to appear in all seven Chronicles)

For when they tried to look at Aslan's face they just caught a glimpse of the golden mane and the great, royal, solemn, overwhelming eyes; and then they found they couldn't look at him and went all trembly.

Aslan, a talking lion, is the creator and guardian of Narnia. He is the son of the great Emperor-beyond-the-Sea. Aslan is powerful, but he is also wise, gentle, and compassionate. He is the most important of all the characters in the Narnia books because—and this is the big secret— he represents Jesus! He is the only character to appear in all seven of the books, and he is the only one who can save the worlds. Aslan is there in *The Magician's Nephew* before Narnia begins, and he is there in *The Last Battle* after Old Narnia is destroyed.

There are lots of places in all seven Chronicles where Aslan acts like Jesus did, says something like Jesus said, and treats characters like Jesus treated people. Aslan even had some of the same names that the Bible has for Christ. Here are a few examples:

NAMES OF ASLAN	NAMES OF JESUS
The Lion (all Chronicles)	The Lion of Judah (Revelation 5:5)
High King above all kings (*HHB*)	King of kings (Revelation 17:14)
Lord of the whole wood (*LWW*)	Lord of lords (Revelation 17:14)
Son of the great Emperor-beyond-the-Sea (*LWW*)	Son of God (Matthew 26:63–64)
The Lamb (*VDT*)	The Lamb (Revelation 13:8)
Myself (*HHB*)	I AM (Exodus 3:14)

JUSTIN TIME
Aslan is the Turkish word for "lion."

Aslan first appears in *The Magician's Nephew* when Digory Kirke and Polly Plummer see him creating a new world through song. They hear singing, and sunlight begins to erase the nothingness. Then they see the singer.

It was a lion. Huge, shaggy, and bright, it stood facing the risen sun.

In this scene, Aslan is being revealed as Jesus, who is the Son of God but is also God Himself, part of the three-in-one God known as the Trinity. The Trinity is God the Father, Jesus the Son, and the Holy Spirit. The Bible says that Jesus, who is called the Word, was with God from the beginning.

God
+ Jesus
+ Holy Spirit
Trinity

Before the world began, there was the Word. The Word was with God, and the Word was God. He was with God in the beginning. All things were made through him. Nothing was made without him. (John 1:1-3)

In the garden of Eden, God told Adam to name the animals and take care of them (Genesis 1:26–28; 2:19–20). In Narnia, Aslan chooses two humans—the cabby Frank and his wife, Helen—to be the first King and Queen of Narnia. He tells them to name the creatures, rule over them, and protect them (*MN*).

Jesus was the Word who spoke the world into existence. Aslan was the Singer who sang Narnia into being.

SECRET SIMILARITIES
BETWEEN JESUS AND ASLAN

Jesus created Earth. (Colossians 1:16)

Aslan created Narnia. (*MN*)

Jesus gave His life to save every person who believes in Him.
   (Matthew 27; Mark 15; Luke 23; John 19)

Aslan gave his life for Edmund's. (*LWW*)

Jesus cried when Lazarus was dead. (John 11:35)

Aslan cried about Digory's mother being sick. (*MN*)

Jesus was tempted by Satan. (Mark 1:13; Luke 4:2)

Aslan agreed to meet with the wicked Queen Jadis. (*LWW*)

Jesus has always existed. (Hebrews 13:8)

Aslan told Lucy he calls all times "soon." That means that whether
   something happened a long time ago, took place right then, or
   was going to happen in the future, it was all pretty much the
   same to Aslan, since he has lived and will live forever. (*VDT*)

After Jesus died, He came to life again. (Matthew 28; Mark 16;
   Luke 24; John 20)

After Aslan died, he came to life again. (*LWW*)

Jesus' blood gives everyone who believes in Him eternal life.
   (Hebrews 5:9)

Aslan's blood gave King Caspian eternal life. (*SC*)

Aslan shows clearly in all seven books that, just like Jesus, he knows everything and is all-powerful. More than once, different characters say that Aslan is "not a tame lion." Mr. Beaver tells the Pevensies this in *The Lion, the Witch and the Wardrobe*.

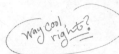

He's wild, you know. Not like a tame lion.

Although Aslan is not a tame lion, he is a good one, Mr. Beaver says. That's another important secret to recognize about Jesus. He is not a jack-in-the-box Jesus who pops up the instant you want Him to or a soda machine Jesus you can pray to and expect the answer you want to fall right in your lap. Sorry, that means you can't pray for a new PlayStation and expect to find it connected to your TV five minutes later. That's not the way it works with Aslan *or* with Jesus. Jesus, like Aslan, is good. He knows the best things for you are not always the things you want.

Aslan knows all the characters better than they know themselves, and he loves them. Jesus has known who you are and what you will grow up to be since before you were even born. Aslan wants the characters and creatures he loves to play with him, talk with him, and let him encourage them. He also corrects them, makes them more grown-up, and hurts when they hurt. That's the kind of relationship Jesus wants to have with you—a best-friends-forever one.

Probably the most important of all, Aslan always forgives the characters when they do the wrong thing. Just like Jesus will always forgive you if you ask Him to.

Way cool, right?

JOSHUA'S JOURNEY

Q: Why does Aslan sometimes go away?

A: Aslan, like Jesus, is always present; but people can't always see or hear him. Many people do not believe in Aslan or don't keep a close relationship with him, so it doesn't seem to them that he exists—or it seems like he is far away. Uncle Andrew in *The Magician's Nephew*, for example, hears Aslan's song as a roar because he refuses to believe. Still, Jesus is always there waiting for people to come closer and believe.

For what you see and hear depends a good deal on where you are standing; it also depends on what sort of person you are.

In *The Horse and His Boy*, Aslan shows Shasta/Prince Cor how much he always cares, just like Jesus cares for us. Aslan describes how he has been with Shasta all through his life. He tells Shasta he was the lion who made him hook up with Aravis, he was the cat who made Shasta feel better at the tombs, and he drove the jackals away while Shasta was sleeping. He also helped Shasta other times too, even way back when he was little. Shasta was never alone or forgotten. Aslan was there.

Shasta was never abandoned, even when he thought nobody cared.

I was the lion who gave the Horses new strength of fear for the last mile so that you should reach King Lune in time. And I was the lion you do not remember who pushed the boat in which you lay, a child near death, so that it came to shore where a man sat, wakeful at midnight, to receive you.

Jesus cares for you the same way. Even when you can't see Him and don't feel Him, He is there. When you unlock the secret that Aslan represents Jesus, you can imagine all the ways that He wants to love, guide, and be there for you.

ASLAN'S SECRET
He stands for Jesus Christ!

UNLOCKING THE SECRET SYMBOLS OF YOUR OWN FAITH

What qualities about Aslan did you like best in the stories?

What qualities do you like best about Jesus?

How have you seen Jesus show up in your own life—like how Aslan was there for Shasta even when Shasta didn't know it?

As You Grow, Your Relationship with Jesus Gets Bigger

Many of the characters and creatures, objects, and places in Narnia contain secret signs of faith. But there are other secrets in the books that will help you learn more about your relationship with Jesus. You can spot these secrets when several characters react the same way or face the same kinds of situations. If you can find these symbols and dive deeper into what they mean, they can help you know Jesus better. In this book, you will uncover seven of Narnia's Greatest Secrets, which point out some lessons of faith you can learn from the Chronicles.

So are you ready to unlock one of Narnia's Greatest Secrets? Are you sure? First, you need to take this quiz:

Instructions: Circle the right answer.

When I feel sad and lonely, I usually:
  a. Eat a lot of ice cream
  b. Cry and feel sorry for myself

more ➔

34

c. Get mad at my little brother

d. Pray and ask Jesus to help me through my hard time

It's easy to see that the answer is supposed to be "d" (although ice cream sounds pretty good too).

It isn't always easy to remember to pray. Aslan teaches the Pevensies, Digory, Eustace, Jill, and other Narnian characters that they can call on him and trust him when they are in trouble. The more they trust Aslan and believe in him, the closer they get to him, the easier it is to see him, and the more they learn about themselves.

Instructions: Circle the right answer.

If I want to get closer to Jesus, I should:

a. Eat more ice cream

b. Watch more TV

c. Talk to Him like I would talk to my friends

d. Read the Bible and hang out with other people who love Him

e. c and d

*The correct answer is "e," but give yourself half credit if you're one of those people who only reads as far as the first right answer and picked "c." (Hint: on school tests, read all the choices.)

Jesus wants you to get close to Him too. When you talk to Jesus about everything, read your Bible, go to church, and hang out with other people who also believe in Jesus, you grow in your relationship with Him.

When Lucy goes back to Narnia in *Prince Caspian*, Aslan calls to her while she is asleep. Lucy's love for Aslan shows because she recognizes his voice as the one she "likes best in the whole world." She runs straight to Aslan, hugging and kissing him, and then tells him he looks bigger. Aslan tells Lucy she thinks he is bigger because she is older now. While Aslan is always the same, every year that Lucy grows, she will discover that Aslan is bigger.

That's the key to unlocking the first of Narnia's Greatest Secrets. When Aslan is talking to Lucy here, he means that Lucy is physically older than she was the last time she saw him. But the secret meaning is that C. S. Lewis is really talking about "growing" in your faith. Every year you grow closer to Jesus, He will seem bigger to you because you will learn more about Him. The more time you spend studying your Bible, praying, and growing in your faith in Jesus, the more real He will seem to you and the more you will see how much He can do to help you experience the life He has for you.

I have good plans for you. I don't plan to hurt you. I plan to give you hope and a good future. Then you will call my name. You will come to me and pray to me. And I will listen to you. You will search for me. And when you search for me with all your heart, you will find me! (Jeremiah 29:11–13)

Peter Pevensie

➤ (*The Lion, the Witch and the Wardrobe*, *Prince Caspian*, and *The Last Battle*)

Peter, by the gift of Aslan, by election, by prescription, and by conquest, High King over all Kings in Narnia, Emperor of the Lone Islands and Lord of Cair Paravel, Knight of the Most Noble Order of the Lion.

Peter Pevensie is the oldest of four children who come from England to the magical world of Narnia, where they are changed forever. That's the secret under the surface of the Pevensies—they had many great adventures and learned from their experiences, so now we can learn from them.

The Pevensies are secret symbols of faith because they learn lessons from Aslan that Jesus wants us to learn in real life. If we look carefully at their actions and choices, we can see the times they make mistakes and the times they grow and get things right. We can watch their relationship with Aslan and (hopefully) avoid making some of their mistakes ourselves.

JUSTIN TIME

When C. S. Lewis was first creating the stories of Narnia, he originally named the four Pevensie children Ann, Martin, Rose, and Peter—and Peter was the youngest.

Peter is the oldest of the four Pevensie kids, and in *The Lion, the Witch and the Wardrobe*, Aslan names him the High King of Narnia. On the surface of the story, Peter is just a boy who becomes a king. Under the surface, the secret to Peter's relationship with Aslan is the honor that should be passed between fathers and sons—and between God and His sons (and daughters).

JUSTIN TIME

It was 1939 when C. S. Lewis had the story idea of four children being sent away from London to a professor's house in the country because of the air raids. But he did not start writing *The Lion, the Witch and the Wardrobe* until ten years later.

Peter looks forward to adventure from the very first pages of *The Lion, the Witch and the Wardrobe* when he and his siblings are sent away from their home in London to the Professor's big, old house in the country. Instead of worrying about what he is leaving behind, Peter looks ahead to the fun they can have exploring the house and gardens. As the oldest, Peter feels responsible for the others. For example, he scolds Edmund for teasing Lucy about Narnia. Later, when Aslan names Peter High King of Narnia, Peter becomes responsible for an entire kingdom. He makes mistakes, feels bad about them, and isn't afraid to say, "I'm sorry" for them. By the end of the book, Peter grows from a boy into an honorable man and royal king.

PETER PEVENSIE
THE GOOD, THE BAD, AND THE UGLY

GOOD PETER	NOT-SO-PERFECT PETER
Acts responsible for his brothers and sisters.	Is afraid of Aslan at first and tries to get Susan to talk to him (*LWW*).
Honors Aslan's authority by raising his sword, even though he's never seen Aslan before and it feels awkward (*LWW*).	At first, he does not believe in what he cannot see. He doesn't believe Lucy found another world in the wardrobe (*LWW*). And Peter loses faith again by not believing that Lucy sees Aslan (*PC*).
Stands up for Edmund and is willing to take responsibility for being angry with Edmund (*LWW*).	Gets frustrated when he has to make hard choices and sometimes doesn't have a good reason for his choices. When the others vote against going Lucy's way, he admits Lucy may be right but still votes the other way (*PC*).
Confronts evil head-on and fights it. He kills Maugrim the Wolf and fights the wicked Witch Jadis (*LWW*).	*more* ➡

GOOD PETER	NOT-SO-PERFECT PETER
Trusts Aslan. When Aslan sends the leopards as messengers to Jadis, Peter says Aslan would not put them in danger (*LWW*).	

In *The Lion, the Witch and the Wardrobe*, Peter's belief in Aslan helps him grow up to be a great warrior called King Peter the Magnificent. Before Aslan is killed by the White Witch, Jadis, he takes Peter aside and gives him instructions on how to manage the troops in battle to defeat the Witch. Aslan put Peter in charge, a lot like Jesus put the disciple Peter in charge of leading the early believers in Christ.

Peter means "rock"

So I tell you, you are Peter. And I will build my church on this rock. The power of death will not be able to defeat my church. (Matthew 16:18)

PETER'S SECRET

If you trust Jesus, He will help you defeat evil in your life, strengthen your faith, and use you to do great things!

Uncovering the Secret Symbols of Your Own Faith

If your brother or sister said they had discovered another world, how would you find out if it was true or not?

When your faith is put to the test like Peter's was when he had to fight the Witch, how do you handle it?

Peter had a lot of responsibility. What responsibilities do you have? Are you handling them the way Jesus wants you to?

Susan Pevensie

→ *(The Lion, the Witch and the Wardrobe, The Horse and His Boy*, and *Prince Caspian)*

Queen Susan is more like an ordinary grown-up lady.

Susan Pevensie probably has the saddest story in all the Narnia books, but it doesn't start out that way. In the beginning, Susan is a great big sister and a loyal follower of Aslan. In *The Lion, the Witch and the Wardrobe*, she is smart and kind. In *The Horse and His Boy*, she is known as a gentle queen. At first Susan does not believe Lucy when Lucy says she has been to Narnia, but she quickly comes around when she enters Narnia through the Wardrobe and meets Aslan. Susan loves the great Lion and is devoted to him, kissing him and crying after the Witch kills him.

JUSTIN TIME

When Susan and Lucy touch Aslan, kiss him, and stroke his fur after he dies, they are a lot like the Bible's two Marys who went to Jesus' tomb to take care of His body (Mark 16:1; Luke 24:1).

After the way Susan loved Aslan, it's hard to believe that she might not end up in Aslan's Country forever with her brothers and sister. After Aslan talks to Peter and Susan at the end of *Prince Caspian*, Peter tells Edmund and Lucy that he and Susan won't be coming back to Narnia. Peter seems sad but understanding. Susan doesn't say anything. The clue to where her heart might be comes on the page before, when Susan focuses on how silly they will look if they return to England in their royal robes and jewels.

 "Nice fools we'd look on the [train] platform of an English station in these," Susan says and seems to want her plain, old school clothes back.

Another clue to the secret state of Susan's heart comes when the Pevensies arrive in Narnia in *Prince Caspian* and discover that the ruins are their castle, Cair Paravel. Susan doesn't remember it at all.

 "How could I forget?" Susan says when Peter reminds her that they were kings and queens who once sat in the castle's great hall.

Susan seems to be like a seed that fell on stony ground in the story Jesus told in Matthew 13. In Jesus' story, some seeds fell on rich ground and grew strong, some fell away from the soil and did not grow at all, some fell among thorny weeds and got choked out, and some fell on stony ground and quickly grew, then withered away. Susan is like one of those seeds in stony ground. She hears and responds to Aslan, and she quickly grows in her faith and love for Aslan, but then she turns away and forgets him once he is out of her everyday life back in England.

And what is the seed that fell on rocky ground? That seed is like the person who hears the teaching and quickly accepts it with joy. But he does not let the teaching go deep into his life. He keeps it only a short time. (Matthew 13:20–21)

JOSHUA'S JOURNEY

Q: Is Susan really left out of Aslan's Country forever? Isn't that mean of Aslan?

A: At the end of *The Last Battle*, all the others from England (Digory, Polly, Peter, Edmund, Lucy, and the Pevensies' mom and dad) are in Aslan's Country because they died on earth in a train crash. Susan is evidently still living, so it is possible that later she could be sorry for losing her faith and start believing again. Just like Jesus would with us, Aslan would forgive Susan and bring her to his country when she dies on earth. If Susan chooses to not believe again, it is her choice that keeps her out of Aslan's Country, not Aslan's. He won't force anyone to believe in him, just like Jesus never forces us to believe in Him. It's a choice each person has to make.

In *The Horse and His Boy*, Prince Corin gives a hint that Susan is not as deeply rooted in Narnia (and willing to fight for her faith) as her siblings. As Shasta and Corin ride off with Edmund and Lucy to battle the Calormenes, Corin says Queen Susan is back at the castle. He says she is not like her sister, and she doesn't go to war. He tells Shasta that Susan is more like an "ordinary" woman who is all grown-up.

In *Prince Caspian*, Susan admits she really believed that Lucy saw Aslan but she pretended she didn't because she didn't want to follow him. She wants to do things her own way, and in the end, everyone ends up in Aslan's Country but Susan.

When King Tirian asks where Susan is in *The Last Battle*, Peter says Susan is not a friend of Narnia anymore. Eustace says that when the others talk about Narnia, Susan dismisses their memories as children's games. Jill then says Susan is only interested in "nylons and lipstick and invitations." Susan is so caught up in her life in England that it seems she wants nothing to do with the idea of living in Aslan's Country forever.

Think of it like this: When your faith is new, it is kind of like a seed that you plant. You have to water it and put it in a pot with good dirt for it to grow. Once your plant starts to grow, you can't just stick it in a corner and forget about it. No, you have to keep watering it, *Good gardeners are said to have a "green thumb"* give it some fertilizer, and put it in a bigger pot as it grows. You have to take care of your plant all the time for it to grow like it should—just like you have to take care of your faith in Jesus every day to help it grow.

Susan's Secret

Like many people, Susan's faith starts out strong when she is young, but when she grows up, she thinks that Aslan is just a bunch of kids' nonsense. As an adult, Susan wants to do her own thing and thinks she is too "smart" to believe in God anymore. Your faith in God may be strong now, but you need to take care of it and keep it growing so that it will stay strong all your life.

Uncovering the Secret Symbols of Your Own Faith

Are you more like Susan or Peter in your faith in Jesus? How?

How does it make you feel that Susan is not a friend of Narnia anymore?

After considering Susan's example, what will you do differently in your life?

Edmund Pevensie

➤ *(The Lion, the Witch and the Wardrobe, The Horse and His Boy, Prince Caspian, The Voyage of the Dawn Treader, and The Last Battle)*

Edmund was a graver and quieter man than Peter, and great in council and judgment. He was called King Edmund the Just.

Edmund is the third Pevensie sibling, and in the beginning of *The Lion, the Witch and the Wardrobe*, he's the most rotten. He treats his siblings badly, grumbles about the rain, and makes fun of Lucy when she says she went to Narnia. He seems to like being mean just to be mean. That's what leads us to discover that Edmund is another secret symbol of faith we can unlock. Edmund is so bad at the beginning of this book that it is his heart and faith we get to see change the most by the end.

JUSTIN TIME

Turkish Delight, the candy Edmund loves, is a jellied candy made with powdered sugar, cornstarch, cream of tartar, rosewater, and sugar, and can include orange juice, chopped toasted almonds or pistachios.

47

When Edmund stumbles into Narnia for the first time, he quickly becomes the follower of the evil Queen Jadis (the White Witch) because she magically gives him candy that he loves, and she promises to make him a king who is higher than his brother and sisters. She appeals to Edmund's pride and greed, and he falls for it.

Commandment #9

You must not tell lies.

Exodus 20:16

Edmund makes matters worse when he goes back through the wardrobe and lies about going to Narnia. But his lie is quickly discovered when all four Pevensies find themselves in Narnia. Instead of being sorry for what he's done, Edmund continues to want to follow the Witch (and get more candy), and he sneaks away from his siblings and the Beavers to find her castle.

JUSTIN TIME

Peter, Susan, and Lucy eat two meals with Mr. and Mrs. Beaver in *The Lion, the Witch and the Wardrobe*, but Edmund only eats the first one. At the Beaver home, the meal includes trout, potatoes, milk, butter, marmalade rolls, and tea. The meal Edmund misses in the secret cave consists of lump sugar, tea, ham sandwiches, and a jug of cream.

When he gets there, he discovers that the Queen's promises—just like the devil's promises in real life—are all a bunch of lies. She kidnaps Edmund and is about to kill him when Aslan has some of his animals rescue Edmund. Edmund's heart changes when he comes face-to-face with Aslan the Lion. Aslan talks to Edmund, and he is completely changed—forever.

There is no need to tell you (and no one ever heard) what Aslan was saying, but it was a conversation which Edmund never forgot.

Edmund apologizes to everyone and shows up in four more of the Chronicles (more than any other human except Lucy). In all of these, he is an important and popular king, and no one ever mentions the way he used to act (except when he brings it up himself to make Eustace feel better in *The Voyage of the Dawn Treader* and when he indirectly mentions it in *The Horse and His Boy*). His old behavior is forgiven and forgotten, and once he begins to believe in Aslan, he is a new man, just like everyone who believes in Jesus becomes new inside.

Because Edmund understands how fair and good Aslan is to him, he becomes wise in giving advice and judging situations. He becomes known as King Edmund the Just. In *Prince Caspian*, Aslan tells Edmund, "You did well," just like Jesus said in the story He told about the servants and their master.

The master answered, "You did well. You are a good servant who can be trusted. You did well with small things. So I will let you care for much greater things. Come and share my happiness with me." (Matthew 25:23)

Edmund's Secret

When Edmund decides to stop following the Queen and puts his faith in Aslan, his life changes. He asks to be forgiven, and his heart is softened. When you decide to stop doing wrong things and ask Jesus to forgive you, Jesus will change your heart forever too.

Unlocking the Secret Symbols of Your Own Faith

When the evil White Witch first calls to Edmund, he doesn't want to go to her but he "dared not disobey" (*LWW*). Why? How might Edmund's life have been different if he had run for the wardrobe or refused to go to the Witch?

How does your life go when you make good choices? What happens to you when you make bad ones?

Describe a time when you asked Jesus to forgive you and how you felt after you did it.

Lucy Pevensie

➤ (*The Lion, the Witch and the Wardrobe, The Horse and His Boy, Prince Caspian, The Voyage of the Dawn Treader,* and *The Last Battle*)

Lucy was a very truthful girl.

Lucy is the youngest of the four Pevensie children, but she is not spoiled or babyish. In fact, she is the most faithful and loyal to Narnia and the one who loves Aslan the most. The secrets to unlock about Lucy—and they are really important—are how she stands strong in her belief that Narnia and Aslan are real and how much she really, truly loves the great Lion. Lucy isn't always perfect, but she tries the hardest to live what she believes.

JUSTIN TIME

C. S. Lewis had a goddaughter named Lucy Barfield. He dedicated *The Lion, the Witch and the Wardrobe* to her.

Lucy shows right away that she is imaginative, because she is the only one who wants to know what is inside the wardrobe. In *The Lion, the Witch and the Wardrobe*, she opens the door and becomes the first human in that book to enter Narnia.

Faith means being sure of the things we hope for. And faith means knowing that something is real even if we do not see it. (Hebrews 11:1)

She also easily believes and accepts the new world and Aslan as the ruler of it—and of her. In *Prince Caspian*, Lucy hears Aslan's call in the night and is the only one who can see him for a while. In *The Voyage of the Dawn Treader*, Lucy is the only one to call out to Aslan for help when the ship is stuck in the darkness. She delights in Aslan, running and playing with him, and she can't wait for the times when she will see him again.

Imagine playing with a HUGE Lion!

JUSTIN TIME

In Narnia, humans are called the Sons of Adam and Daughters of Eve, because in the Bible the first man God created was Adam and the first woman was Eve.

THINGS TO LOVE ABOUT LUCY

She is friendly and happy.

She is very truthful and never changes her story, even when no one believes her.

She easily accepts what is hard to understand.

She stands for what she believes in, even when it makes her miserable.

She sees beauty in Aslan, even after the Witch shaves off Aslan's mane and the evil creatures beat him.

She knows the most about what Aslan is really like—she sees that he is royal, strong, and peaceful, and she also notices his sadness.

She hurts when others hurt.

She gives freely to others in need (when she heals them with her cordial).

She is humble enough to apologize quickly (and mean it) when she does something wrong.

She respects authority (by reminding Trumpkin in *Prince Caspian* that Peter is the king and they should listen to him).

She doesn't say, "I told you so" or rub it in when she is right and others are wrong.

She always believes in Aslan.

She listens to Aslan.

Now, Lucy isn't perfect. She sometimes snaps at her siblings, and she disobeys Aslan in *Prince Caspian* when she goes with the others instead of following the Lion. But her faith and actions are great secrets to uncover, because Lucy can teach you what truly following Jesus with all of your heart looks like. Because Lucy stays the closest to Aslan, she knows him the best, and she experiences the most joy.

LUCY'S SECRET

She really, truly loves Aslan, the way you should really, truly love Jesus—like He's your very best friend. Lucy understands what it means to have faith, and she proves it in the way she lives every day.

UNLOCKING THE SECRET SYMBOLS OF YOUR OWN FAITH

What would you do if Jesus walked in your front door today? How would you feel?

Name a time when you knew the right thing to do and did it, even when other kids were not doing it.

What are some of the things you can do to make Jesus your best friend?

Prince Caspian (King Caspian X, The King of Old Narnia)

 (Prince Caspian, The Voyage of the Dawn Treader, The Silver Chair, and The Last Battle)

> *You are the true King of Narnia: Caspian the Tenth, the true son and heir of Caspian the Ninth. Long life to your Majesty.*

Prince Caspian becomes King of Narnia nearly one thousand Narnia years after Aslan makes the four Pevensie children the Kings and Queens of Narnia. Caspian's father was King Caspian IX, a Telmarine who was killed by his brother Miraz. Miraz takes over as king and raises the rightful heir to the throne. (The Telmarines conquered Narnia hundreds of Narnia years ago.)

JUSTIN TIME

An ancient Narnia prophecy says that only humans can be Kings of Narnia. Caspian's family comes from human pirates who lived long ago and fell through a crack between earth and the land that became Telmar. The pirates eventually became the Telmarines, who conquered Narnia.

The young Caspian X does not know that his uncle murdered his dad or that he is the rightful king. Many Narnians no longer believe in Aslan, and most of the Talking Animals are gone or in hiding. The castle Cair Paravel lies in ruins.

When he is young, Caspian's nurse tells him stories of Old Narnia and Aslan the Lion, and Caspian believes them. Miraz hates the stories, dismisses the nurse, and hires a tutor, Doctor Cornelius. But Doctor Cornelius is also an Old Narnian, and Caspian continues to hear the stories and believe. When his aunt and uncle have a baby boy, the young Prince Caspian has to run for his life and fight Miraz's army to reclaim the throne and get Narnia back on the right track following Aslan.

JUSTIN TIME

The words *belief* and *believed* appear about thirty times in the book *Prince Caspian*.

Caspian's secret is that he, like Lucy, knows what it means to have faith. In fact, the young Caspian has more faith than Lucy, in a way, because he believes in Aslan long before he ever sees him. Caspian has only heard stories about Aslan; he has never seen him. But his heart still responds and knows the truth.

Believe in the Lord Jesus and you will be saved. (Acts 16:31)

While fighting Miraz's army, Caspian blows Susan's ivory horn and believes that it will bring help. (It does; it calls the Pevensies back to Narnia.) Caspian and his army are losing, and a Dwarf named Nikabrik tells Caspian to stop believing in Aslan and to allow the Witch's power to help them. Caspian doesn't even consider it. His belief in Aslan remains strong, even though no one has seen Aslan in Narnia for hundreds of years—and even though nothing seems to be going Caspian's way.

Caspian is still a young man during this war, and he is a brand-new king. He is not experienced in fighting battles or running a country yet, but he is wise enough to have faith. Because of this faith, Aslan returns, Miraz is defeated, and the Old Narnians are free to live in peace again for a while.

In *The Voyage of the Dawn Treader*, King Caspian sails east to try to find seven friends of his father whom Miraz sent away. Along the way, Caspian becomes a more mature, powerful king. He gets rid of slavery on the Lone Islands and puts a good governor in power, overcomes his own greed at Goldwater Island, and meets his future wife, the daughter of Ramandu the star. At the end of the book, Caspian decides that he wants to go with Reepicheep to Aslan's Country instead of sailing back to Narnia.

Edmund tells Caspian he can't go, and Caspian gets angry. He doesn't like being bossed around. Reepicheep reminds Caspian about the things he is supposed to do as King of Narnia, and Caspian stomps off to his cabin. Aslan magically appears and talks to Caspian, and Caspian knows he must go back to Narnia and do the right thing. He later gets to go to Aslan's Country when he dies a very old king in *The Silver Chair*. After he dies, Aslan's blood changes Caspian back into a young man who lives forever.

Caspian believes in Aslan all his life, and along the way he learns lessons about responsibility and doing things that don't seem much fun but are the right things to do. Jesus wants us to learn these lessons too. There are many times in life when doing the right thing is hard. And the things you are supposed to do seem a lot less exciting than what you want to do. But

You can make a difference in history, too, when you do the things Jesus expects you to do.

anybody can do things that seem fun. You show people you are different by doing with a good attitude the things you don't want to do. By obeying and believing, Caspian made a positive difference in Narnia for a long, long time.

JOSHUA'S JOURNEY

Q: Why can't Caspian go with Reepicheep into Aslan's Country?

A: If Caspian went with Reepicheep, he would get to experience the great joy of Aslan's Country; but the country he is ruling, which still needs him, would suffer. Aslan knows Caspian will join him in his country someday, but it is not the right time yet. You were created with certain things to do here on earth and a specific time to meet Jesus in heaven if you believe in Him, but only He knows the right time. You are not supposed to try to go to heaven sooner than God wants you to.

CASPIAN'S SECRET

Faith is super-important for a successful life. In order to be fully grown-up, sometimes you have to do things that are hard and that you don't want to do—and do them with a good attitude.

Unlocking the Secret Symbols
of Your Own Faith

What are two things you hate to do but you have to do anyway?
What do you think you are supposed to learn by doing them?

Why do you think Caspian was able to keep believing in Aslan
even though no one had seen Aslan for hundreds of years?

How hard is it for you to always believe that Jesus came and
died for you, when you can't see Him or hear Him?

Digory Kirke

 (The Lion, the Witch and the Wardrobe, The Magician's Nephew, and The Last Battle)

 "This is the Boy," said Aslan, looking, not at Digory, but at his councillors. "This is the Boy who did it."

Without Digory Kirke's mistakes and also his bravery, you might never have heard of Narnia. As a boy in *The Magician's Nephew*, Digory leaves England by wearing a magic ring and lands in a place where he gets to see Aslan creating Narnia. Digory's wacky Uncle Andrew has been experimenting with magic, and he tricks Polly into putting on a magic ring first. She disappears, and Digory overcomes his fear of the unknown and also puts on a magic ring to go get Polly and bring her back.

JUSTIN TIME

On July 21, 1998, Great Britain introduced a new series of stamps called "Magical Worlds" that featured a twenty-six-pence stamp of *The Lion, the Witch and the Wardrobe* (and a twenty-pence stamp of J. R. R. Tolkien's *The Hobbit*).

What Polly and Digory discover is that there are other worlds besides theirs. Some are old and dying, while others are not even created yet.

They meet Aslan, the creator of Narnia, and he changes their lives.

Digory's secret is that it often takes courage to do what is right. When you are brave in hard situations, you become a little bit wiser each time. Digory faces temptation several times; when the evil Witch tempts him with the thing he wants the most, Digory looks her right in the face and says no!

Way to go, Digs.

Digory has the chance to be brave many times in *The Magician's Nephew*. He has courage to walk through the ruins in the dying world of Charn. He is brave when he grabs the Witch's leg to get her out of London. He is especially brave when he resists her temptation in the garden. The Witch tells him that if he eats an apple, he will live forever and rule the whole world, but Digory refuses:

No thanks . . . I'd rather live an ordinary time and die and go to Heaven.

JOSHUA'S JOURNEY

Q: How does Digory become so brave, and how can I be brave like him?

A: Digory's courage appears when he does something to save someone else, and it grows each time he faces something he is afraid of. When Polly might be in danger in another world, Digory thinks of her instead of himself and puts on the ring. When the Witch tempts Digory to eat the apple, he has the courage to resist her. When you think of other people instead of yourself, it is easier to have courage.

Digory is brave, but he also has faults, of course. He is selfish and insists on having his own way when he and Polly see the enchanted people of Charn sitting around the table. He wants to ring the bell, and Polly doesn't want him to. He does it anyway, and the evil Witch named Jadis awakens and eventually enters the brand-new world of Narnia.

JUSTIN TIME

Jadis, in French, means "long ago." Since Jadis lives for more than a thousand Narnia years, that name certainly fits.

Aslan talks to Digory about his mistake and gives him a job to do. Digory is to pick a certain life-giving apple as a way to make things right. Digory obeys, and his obedience helps protect Narnia for the next thousand years. Aslan plants the apple in the new Narnia, and it grows overnight into a tree that protects the country from the Witch. Aslan also rewards Digory's obedience by giving him an apple from the new tree to take back to London. Digory feeds it to his dying mother, and she is healed.

When Digory is grown, he becomes a wise professor—the same professor whose house the Pevensie children visit. We discover that Digory made the wardrobe that the Pevensies later traveled through to Narnia out of wood from the apple tree that grew from the core of the life-giving apple Aslan gave him. We also learn that Digory still believes in Narnia, and his faith and obedience are rewarded in *The Last Battle* when he becomes Lord Digory and lives forever in Aslan's Country.

You can follow sin, or obey God. Sin brings spiritual death. But obeying God makes you right with him. (Romans 6:16)

DIGORY'S SECRET

Obeying Jesus and thinking of others more than yourself helps give you courage, and it also has great rewards!

UNLOCKING THE SECRET SYMBOLS OF YOUR OWN FAITH

What do you think would have happened if Digory had eaten the apple that Jadis tempted him to eat?

What are some good things that happened to you when you were brave and obeyed God?

Eustace Scrubb

 (The Voyage of the Dawn Treader, The Silver Chair, and The Last Battle)

There was a boy called Eustace Clarence Scrubb, and he almost deserved it.

Eustace Clarence Scrubb is the very irritating cousin who picks on Edmund and Lucy when they visit him one summer in *The Voyage of the Dawn Treader*. Eustace brags and annoys, and he teases them when they talk about Narnia. The teasing ends when he and Edmund and Lucy suddenly get pulled into Narnia through a picture of the *Dawn Treader* that Eustace's mother has hanging in a back room of their house. Eustace's whole life changes for good when he enters Narnia.

JUSTIN TIME

The picture of the *Dawn Treader* that Edmund, Lucy, and their cousin Eustace are pulled through in *The Voyage of the Dawn Treader* is a wedding present that Edmund's mother hates but didn't get rid of because she doesn't want to hurt the giver's feelings.

The secret symbol of faith in Eustace is that he quits trying to control things and gives himself completely to Aslan. Here's what changes him: After grumbling, complaining, and threatening every day of the voyage, when the *Dawn Treader* stops at an island, Eustace decides to go off on his own so that he doesn't have to do any work. He finds a dragon's cave and decides to take as much of its treasure as he can. But after he spends the night in the cave, Eustace wakes up to find that he has been turned into a dragon!

 . . . *with greedy, dragonish thoughts in his heart, he had become a dragon himself.*

Eustace the dragon returns to the others and gets them to realize that it's him. He is miserable as a dragon, but through his misery his heart changes. He starts helping by catching food, warming people on cold nights, and letting them have rides on his back as he flies them around. He learns to like people.

Six nights later, Aslan appears to Eustace and says to follow him. Eustace does, and Aslan takes him to a garden with a well. He tells Eustace to undress and get in the water. Eustace peels off the dragon skin, only to find that there is another dragon skin underneath! He does this three times before Aslan tells him that he will have to let Aslan undress him. Eustace says the first time Aslan pierced his dragon skin, it felt like it went straight to his heart. It hurts like crazy, but Eustace lets Aslan finish tearing the skin. When it's over, Eustace is himself again—only better. After Eustace decides to follow Aslan, Aslan takes away his dragon skin and throws him in the water. Then Aslan dresses him.

Accurate since it changes Eustaces (?)

Get up, be baptized, and wash your sins away. (Acts 22:16)

This story clearly shows how Jesus makes us new when we give ourselves to Him. After we decide to follow Jesus, He takes away our sins and we are baptized to show our faith in Him. Eustace starts becoming a nicer person from the day he is washed clean. He still makes mistakes sometimes, but "the cure had begun" (*VDT*).

In the first chapter of the next book, *The Silver Chair*, Eustace is back at school in England, and his classmate Jill Pole says everyone is noticing the change in him. The more mature Eustace goes back to Narnia with Jill in *The Silver Chair* and helps save King Caspian's son, Prince Rilian, from a Witch. He also fights bravely to save Narnia from evil in *The Last Battle.* There, Eustace's change from total brat to brave hero is complete, and he walks through the door to live forever in Aslan's Country.

EUSTACE'S SECRET

When you are willing to give yourself to Jesus, He will make you clean from sin. It will hurt to give up some of your old, bad habits, but then Jesus can use you to make a difference in a lot of awesome places.

UNLOCKING THE SECRET SYMBOLS
OF YOUR OWN FAITH

How would it feel if you woke up and discovered you were a dragon? What do you think you would do?

What do you think makes Eustace start being nicer to people after he is turned into a dragon?

Have you made the choice to obey Jesus by letting Him take off your "dragon skin"? Have you been baptized? Ask your parents to help you learn more about getting baptized in water.

Jill Pole

→ (*The Silver Chair* and *The Last Battle*)

"Are you not thirsty?" said the Lion.
"I'm dying of thirst," said Jill.

In the first chapter of *The Silver Chair*, Jill Pole and Eustace Scrubb are at school, and Eustace sees Jill crying after the school bullies have been picking on her. He tells her about Narnia and wonders if they could try to get there. Jill and Eustace scramble up the slope of shrubs around the schoolyard to the high stone wall that opens onto the moor and find that the door that is usually locked is open.

JUSTIN TIME

A moor is an open, wet, and spongy field or piece of land covered with grasses and sedges. England is famous for having moors.

Instead of walking out onto the moor, Eustace and Jill walk through the door and find themselves at the top of a cliff on Aslan's Mountain. Eustace tells Jill she is too close to the edge, but she doesn't like to be told what to do and gets even closer. To save her from falling, Eustace

moves toward her—and falls off the cliff himself.
Aslan suddenly appears and saves Eustace, blowing

Scary

him west toward Narnia. Jill thinks she is dreaming and is afraid.
She wishes she had never come with Eustace, and she denies even to herself that Eustace's fall was her fault. She has a good cry and gets very thirsty
but is afraid to drink from a stream she sees because a lion is resting on
the banks. The lion, of course, is Aslan—but Jill doesn't know that yet.

Jill's secret symbol of faith is the change that occurs in her life when
she gives up her pride and her fear and drinks the water that Aslan offers,
just like what happened when Jesus told the woman at the well that He
was "living water" that would keep her from ever being thirsty again.

Jesus said, "You don't know what God gives. And you don't know who asked
you for a drink. If you knew, you would have asked me, and I would have
given you living water. . . . Every person who drinks this water will be
thirsty again. But whoever drinks the water I give will never be thirsty
again. (John 4:10, 13)

At first, Jill refuses to drink because she is afraid the Lion will get her.

Yikes!
She asks him to go away, but he won't. She asks him if he
eats little girls, and he tells her he has swallowed girls,
boys, adults, cities, and kingdoms! Jill says she will go
look for another place to drink, and Aslan tells her this is the only place,
and she will die of thirst if she doesn't drink.

JOSHUA'S JOURNEY

Q: What does Aslan mean when he says he has swallowed people and whole cities?

A: It means that there are people and places who have gotten so close to Jesus that they give everything to Him. They are not afraid to give up what they want for what Jesus wants. They live their lives "swallowed up" by Him because they ask Jesus what He wants for them instead of planning their lives without Him. Giving everything to Jesus is a really hard thing to do, and it can be scary, but it's a good thing too.

Finally, Jill gives up, kneels down (a sign that she humbles herself before Aslan), and takes a drink.

It was the coldest, most refreshing water she had ever tasted. You didn't need to drink much of it, for it quenched your thirst at once. Before she tasted it she had been intending to make a dash away from the Lion the moment she had finished. Now, she realized that this would be on the whole the most dangerous thing of all.

After she does, she and Aslan start a relationship. Aslan calls her to him, and she confesses that Eustace fell because she was showing off. Aslan then tells her she and Eustace were called to Narnia to save the lost Prince Rilian, and he says the job will be harder for her because of her

actions on the cliff. He gives Jill four signs that will
lead her to the prince and then blows her to Narnia.

Whee! I'm flying on Lion's breath!

In Narnia, Jill and Eustace meet again, and Jill must
remember the signs Aslan gave her and follow his direc-
tions to search for the prince. She learns (sometimes
the hard way, like when she, Eustace, and the Marsh-wiggle Puddleglum
almost get eaten by giants) that life is better when she does things Aslan's
way instead of her own. She also hears and sees how hard life became
for the gnomes in Underland after they gave their lives to the Witch and
lived under her spell. The gnome Golg tells Eustace, Jill, and Rilian how
they lost their joy, their songs, and even their voices as they slaved their
lives away.

JUSTIN TIME

In *The Silver Chair*, the gnome Golg talks about how
the gnomes lost all their joy and says he hasn't let
off a "squib" for a very long time. A squib is a small explosive
device that resembles a tiny stick of dynamite.

Jesus wants you to give Him your life too. You just have to ask Him to
show you what He wants you to do. Ask Him to let you know when you
are not doing what He wants you to do. You might not hear Him speak
out loud to you, but if you keep talking to Him and asking Him to show
you the right things, soon you will recognize the peace that comes with
making the right choices.

Whoever wants to save his life will give up true life. And whoever gives up his life for me will have true life. (Matthew 16:25)

JILL'S SECRET

The only way to find what you are looking for is to give up your whole life—your dreams, the things you love, and your plans—to Jesus and ask Him to give you what He wants you to have. When Jill finally takes a drink of water and does what Aslan asks her to do, her heart changes.

UNLOCKING THE SECRET SYMBOLS OF YOUR OWN FAITH

It is hard to do what other people want you to do, especially when you want to do your own thing. Describe a time when you did not listen to someone you should have listened to and things went wrong.

Have you ever asked Jesus to take your whole life and only give you the dreams He has for you? If not, would you be willing to do that now? How do you think it will feel?

Nobody's Perfect, but You Are Loved

Welcome to the Secret Society of Perfect People. If you have never told a lie, disobeyed your parents, had a bad attitude, said a bad word, hurt your little sister, fought over who gets the front seat in the car, talked back to your mom, cheated on a school paper, thought a bad thought about someone, felt like you hated somebody, left a mess for someone else to clean up, or neglected your dog, you can become an official member of the club!

So are you in? I didn't think so. In fact, no one can be perfect. The Bible says everyone has done something wrong at some point, and most of us do things that are wrong every single day!

All people have sinned and are not good enough for God's glory. (Romans 3:23)

The second of Narnia's Greatest Secrets is that C. S. Lewis shows over and over again in these books that nobody is perfect, but Aslan loves them anyway. That's so cool, when you remember that Aslan stands for Jesus—and that means Jesus loves you no matter what! In the Chronicles, Edmund betrays Aslan to the White Witch, Peter doesn't believe that Lucy sees Aslan, Digory rings the bell and brings evil into Narnia, Jill causes Eustace to fall over the cliff, Prince Rilian falls for the Witch, and Eustace is so nasty to everybody that he ends up as a dragon! Everywhere you turn in Narnia, characters mess up.

That's the key to this secret: messing up is okay if you are sorry and willing to humbly admit that you were wrong. Then, pick yourself up and try again. Once the characters take these steps, they end up better off than they were before.

 It would be nice, and fairly nearly true, to say that "from that time forth, Eustace was a different boy." To be strictly accurate, he began to be a different boy.

Once you admit to Jesus that you have messed up, your life will change too. You still won't be perfect, but your "cure," as *The Voyage of the Dawn Treader* says about Eustace, will have begun. The change won't happen overnight, but it will be a good start. And that's a secret you don't have to keep—pass it on!

If anyone belongs to Christ, then he is made new. The old things have gone; everything is made new! (2 Corinthians 5:17)

Shasta/Prince Cor

→ (*The Horse and His Boy* and *The Last Battle*)

"Apparently King Lune is my father," said Shasta. "I might really have guessed it. Corin being so like me. We were twins, you see. Oh, and my name isn't Shasta, it's Cor."

Shasta, who is also Prince Cor of Archenland, is the main character in *The Horse and His Boy*. Shasta was kidnapped as a baby, found drifting in a boat, and adopted by a Calormen fisherman who put him to work as a slave. Shasta and a Talking Horse named Bree run away together to Narnia to become free from their masters. Along the way, Shasta finds out he is really a prince of a country named Archenland. He is one of King Lune's twin sons who has been missing since he was a baby.

JUSTIN TIME

C. S. Lewis was offered knighthood by Sir Winston Churchill, but he turned it down.

Shasta is young and inexperienced when he starts on the journey. He doesn't even know how to get on a horse, let alone ride it. He isn't sure what he is looking for or where he is going. And that takes us to Shasta's secret symbol of faith: people who are searching for their true purpose in life succeed when they keep looking until they find it. They keep trying until they get it right. Shasta spends most of the book seeking his place in life, and he learns and grows along the way. Finally, he gets face-to-face with Aslan, and when he sees him for the first time—even though he had never even heard of Aslan before—Shasta recognizes that he has found what he has been looking for. As soon as he sees Aslan's face, he slips off the horse and falls at Aslan's feet.

But after one glance at the Lion's face he slipped out of the saddle and fell at its feet. He couldn't say anything but then he didn't want to say anything, and he knew he needn't say anything. The High King above all kings stooped toward him.

After Shasta meets Aslan and talks with him, Aslan walks away. His footprints mysteriously fill with water, and Shasta drinks the water. Here, another character in the Chronicles has discovered Aslan's "living water," one of the Bible's descriptions of Jesus. From then on, Shasta is a friend and follower of Aslan, and he later finds out that he is a prince.

Better than Gatorade!

On that day Jesus stood up and said in a loud voice, "If anyone is thirsty, let him come to me and drink. If a person believes in me, rivers of living water will flow out from his heart." (John 7:37–38)

JOSHUA'S JOURNEY

Q: How does Shasta's story about being a prince have anything to do with me and Jesus?

A: After Shasta meets and believes in Aslan, he finds his earthly father, King Lune, and discovers he is the son of this important king. Jesus is described in the Bible as the King of kings, and those who love Him become His "sons and daughters." So, if you are a believer in Jesus, you are royalty too!

"I will be your Father, and you will be my sons and daughters," says the Lord All-Powerful. (2 Corinthians 6:18)

SHASTA'S SECRET

When Shasta looks faithfully for what he is missing and keeps persevering along the way, he finds a relationship with Aslan and his place in a royal family. If you feel like something is missing in your life, remember that you can give your heart to your Father, God, and be part of a royal family too!

UNLOCKING THE SECRET SYMBOLS
OF YOUR OWN FAITH

If you had never heard about Jesus, do you think you could believe in Him if someone told you about Him?

What evidence of Aslan did Shasta see and hear before meeting him?

When you meet Jesus for the first time in heaven, what do you think that will be like? What do you think you will do?

Aravis

➤ *(The Horse and His Boy and The Last Battle)*

In this idea about Aravis Shasta was quite wrong. She was proud and could be hard enough but she was true as steel and would never have deserted a companion, whether she liked him or not.

Aravis is a young noblewoman of Calormen in *The Horse and His Boy* who runs away from her father because he is forcing her to marry a mean, old man. Aravis is stubborn and proud, and she runs away to Narnia on her horse, Hwin. On her way, she meets Shasta and his horse, Bree. Shasta and Aravis don't get along at first, but their horses do, since Hwin is also a Talking Horse from Narnia. The four decide they will be less likely to get caught as runaways if they travel together, and they set off for Narnia, where they have heard they can be free.

Aravis is different from most of the humans in Narnia because she comes from a land that absolutely does not believe in Aslan. In fact, the Calormenes give all their loyalty to the Tisroc (who is like a king in Calormen) and think that Aslan is a demon. Aravis's secret symbol of faith is the complete turnaround she has to do to believe in Aslan.

Aravis has heard about Aslan, but the stories she has heard are the exact opposite of what Aslan really is. She has to go from being against Aslan to being *for* him, while other characters just have to go from a place of believing nothing about Aslan to finding a relationship with him. In the book, Aravis changes from being fiercely loyal to the Tisroc to believing in Aslan.

Most of the characters in Narnia have never heard of Aslan, so they have not decided beforehand whether they should believe in him or not.

JOSHUA'S JOURNEY

Q: I have a friend who doesn't want to believe in Jesus. How can I tell him what Jesus is really like?

A: You could see if your friend wants to read The Chronicles of Narnia and talk about them, and you could even give him a copy of this book. But the best way you can help your friend see what Jesus is really like is to *show* him, not tell him. If you are loving and kind and honest, your friend may want to know what makes you different. Then you can say that the reason is your love for Jesus. If you try to talk about Jesus and friends do not want to listen, stop talking about Him. Then pray for your friends every day. It is Jesus' job to knock on the door of your friends' hearts, and it's your friends' job to open the door. Your job is just to keep living for Jesus in a way that is contagious (kinda like a cold—your faith should rub off on everybody around you!).

A wicked fool says to himself, "There is no God." (Psalm 14:1)

Aravis is the only character Aslan hurts in order to help her see where she went wrong. Aslan slashes Aravis's back with his claws and later tells her that the ten scratches represent the ten lashes with a whip that a maid got when Aravis ran away. Aravis's transformation has to be painful to be real. It can't come too easily, or she might change her mind and believe in something else later. Her faith comes with a price for her sin, and Aravis understands. In the end, Aravis becomes a true believer, marries Shasta (who is now Prince Cor), and reigns as Queen of Narnia.

The Lord corrects those he loves, just as a father corrects the child that he likes. (Proverbs 3:12)

ARAVIS'S SECRET

Even though she had heard the wrong things about Aslan and started out believing in something else, Aravis changes her mind after she meets Aslan. If you have believed in something other than Jesus or not believed in anything at all, Aravis's story shows that it is never too late to put your faith in Jesus, who loves you.

Unlocking the Secret Symbols of Your Own Faith

Who do you know who does not have a relationship with Jesus? Pray for that person every day.

Name three ways you will show your faith in Jesus to others, rather than tell them.

Prince Rilian

→ (*The Silver Chair* and *The Last Battle*)

You may well believe that I know Narnia, for I am Rilian, Prince of Narnia, and Caspian the great King is my father.

Prince Rilian is the son of King Caspian X (formerly Prince Caspian). In *The Silver Chair*, Rilian is put under a spell by a beautiful lady who turns out to be a wicked Witch, the Queen of Underland. The Queen kills Rilian's mother, and when Prince Rilian decides to go into the woods looking for the murderer in order to get even, he meets the wicked Queen instead and is taken underground to Underland.

JUSTIN TIME

C. S. Lewis was part of a writers' group called Inklings. (Get it? They wrote with ink, and if you have an inkling about something, it means you have had an idea or a feeling about something—and writers are always coming up with new ideas.) One of the other members of the group was J. R. R. Tolkien, who wrote The Lord of the Rings books and was C. S. Lewis's good friend.

In Underland, Eustace and Jill eventually find the lost prince under a spell that makes him believe that he is happy about being with the Queen. The Queen has an evil plan to dig a tunnel underneath Narnia, pop up above ground when it is finished, and take over Aslan's kingdom. Rilian seems excited about this plan. For one hour each day, however, the spell over Rilian is broken, and Rilian is able to tell Eustace and Jill who he really is. He also remembers that he does not want to be with the Queen or go along with her evil plan. Eustace and Jill cut Rilian free from his bindings, and when the Queen comes in and turns into a serpent, Rilian kills her.

This is Rilian's secret symbol of faith: that even after being foolish and giving himself over to evil, somewhere inside he can still recognize the truth and finally defeat the evil that keeps him from being free. When you choose to follow Jesus, the Bible says you can beat the evil that is trying to have power over you. You get to make the choice, because no one can rule over your heart if you put your faith in Jesus.

God's Spirit, who is in you, is greater than the devil, who is in the world. (1 John 4:4)

Rilian also shows how a father's faith can make a difference in his children. King Caspian has a very strong belief in Aslan and a desire to follow him, and his son Rilian heard the stories of Aslan all his life. Rilian is able to kill the Queen, who represents evil, because inside he already believes in Aslan.

In the Chronicles, C. S. Lewis uses a lot of bad queens to represent the devil. It's like how the devil takes different forms sometimes, but he is always evil.

The Queen may rule over Underland, but she does not rule over Rilian's heart, even though she fools him for a while. Once he is free of her, Rilian becomes a great King of Narnia.

RILIAN'S SECRET

Even when the devil fools you and you turn away from Jesus, you can come back to Him.

UNLOCKING THE SECRET SYMBOLS OF YOUR OWN FAITH

Can you remember a time when you knew you were about to do the wrong thing, but you did it anyway? What happened? Did you make it right?

How has the faith of someone important to you made a difference in what you believe?

King Tirian

→ *(The Last Battle)*

> *His name was King Tirian, and he was between twenty and twenty-five years old. . . . He had blue eyes and a fearless, honest face.*

King Tirian is the ruler of Narnia when *The Last Battle* begins and when Old Narnia, the one created by Aslan in *The Magician's Nephew*, comes to an end. He is a good king who has kept faith in Aslan, even though Aslan has not been seen for hundreds of years and Narnia is falling apart. When Roonwit the Centaur gives Tirian a message that Aslan has returned to Narnia, Tirian is filled with joy.

Tirian is the last king of Narnia

JUSTIN TIME

In *The Last Battle*, Jill Pole whispers for King Tirian to get down in order to see better by saying, "*Thee better*" because when you are trying to keep someone from hearing you, the sound they are most likely to hear in a whisper is the hissing "s-s-s-s" sound.

Tirian finds out that the reports of Aslan are not good ones. People are saying that Aslan has changed from the all-powerful, loving protector of Narnia into a cruel beast who is now forming a partnership with the unbelieving Calormenes, who want to conquer Narnia and make its creatures into slaves. Tirian does not believe it, but as more stories reach him, he begins to feel sad and worried. Yet, even when things seem to go horribly wrong, Tirian still believes and fights for Aslan. That's when Tirian's secret symbol of faith becomes obvious: his faith is so strong that he will fight for it to the end, no matter what goes wrong.

 Oh no!

Tirian discovers that a bad ape named Shift has created an Aslan lookalike by putting an old lion skin over a silly donkey named Puzzle. Shift fools the Narnians and gets on the good side of the cruel Calormenes by parading this fake Aslan in front of the Narnian animals and creatures each evening and making them obey the fake Aslan.

JOSHUA'S JOURNEY

Q: Why do you think C. S. Lewis put in the part about Digory, Polly, Peter, Edmund, Lucy, Eustace, and Jill visiting together, eating, and talking about Narnia?

A: This is another secret symbol—a picture of the church and our job as believers in Jesus to get together to talk about Jesus, eat together, and learn more about our faith. The book of Acts in the Bible tells what the first people who believed in Jesus did together after Jesus rose from the dead, spent time with them, and then went up to heaven. The believers spent time together, talking about Jesus and eating together. Today, people sometimes call this "fellowship."

King Tirian cannot understand why the animals fall for something that is so obviously a lie. But they do, and even when they discover the truth, many of them still give up their faith in the real Aslan. They are so confused, sad, and angry that they were fooled and that the real Aslan has not shown up in so long that they choose to no longer believe in Aslan at all. They have never seen him, so they decide he must have just been an old legend. Tirian still believes, calls on Aslan for help, and is given a brief peek into the English house where the humans who love Narnia are gathered together. Eustace and Jill appear in Narnia and join in the battle.

Tirian fights for Aslan and Narnia to the very end of *The Last Battle*, when he suddenly finds himself in Aslan's Country. Old Narnia is destroyed, and believers in Aslan are reunited in a new Narnia—a beautiful world that will never end.

TIRIAN'S SECRET

Tirian's strong faith in Aslan—even when everything is going wrong around him and there is no hope in sight—is an example to all believers in Jesus. It should be hard for you to even imagine why anyone would turn away from Jesus, and you should keep following Him even when it feels like nothing is going right or you are the only one who believes in Him.

Unlocking the Secret Symbols of Your Own Faith

After reading in *The Last Battle* C. S. Lewis's version of what heaven might be like, how do you feel about it? Does heaven seem more real to you, like a place you actually want to go to someday?

Do you think you will go to heaven when you die? Find someone you trust to talk to about this.

NARNIA'S GREATEST SECRET NO. 3

Even the Small and Seemingly Unimportant Can Do Mighty Things

Now that you've discovered the secret symbols of faith found in the good Narnian characters, it's time to turn the spotlight on another of Narnia's Greatest Secrets. Are you ready? Okay, let's see if you're really ready. Here's your quiz:

Instructions: Circle the right answer.

In order to do something really great in your life, you have to be:

    a. Superrich

    b. Famous

    c. Willing to do whatever Jesus wants you to do

    d. Good-looking

    e. Tall and strong

more ➤

*Did you pick "c"? You probably did, but do you really believe that? All the magazines and TV shows around you make a big deal out of the rich, the famous, and the beautiful. But Jesus doesn't. And Aslan didn't either.

Even the small and seemingly unimportant creatures are used by Aslan to do great and mighty things. It doesn't matter if you are as small and weak as a mouse; Jesus can use you in powerful ways. There are lots of examples of this in the creatures of Narnia and how they fit into the Chronicles.

Mr. Tumnus

Mr. Tumnus is a good place to start. He is a Faun—part man, part goat. He is nervous and shy around Lucy when he meets her in *The Lion, the Witch and the Wardrobe*. The reason quickly becomes known when he confesses that he is going to turn Lucy in to Jadis, the White Witch. Mr. Tumnus feels sorry for his plans, changes his mind, and is forgiven by Lucy. He is the first example of what it looks like to mess up, say you are sorry, and be forgiven in The Chronicles of Narnia.

Reepicheep

Reepicheep the Mouse is another great example of this secret symbol of faith. He is very little, but he is a mighty warrior willing to fight for what is right. He is the most determined to see Aslan's Country, and he is brave enough to be the first one to get there in *The Voyage of the Dawn Treader*. He is fearless, and his quick thinking saves the *Dawn Treader* from the sea serpent. Reepicheep is always loyal to Aslan and the friends of Narnia.

JUSTIN TIME

Reepicheep comes from the family of mice who gnawed through the ropes that bound Aslan to the Stone Table.

Other Loyal Creatures

In each of the Chronicles, animals and mythical creatures participate in important things. Here are a few examples.

CREATURE	IMPORTANT JOB
Strawberry, the old London cab horse (*MN*)	Aslan changes the horse into Fledge, the first Pegasus. Fledge takes Digory and Polly to get the special apple.
Puddleglum the Marsh-wiggle (*SC*)	Puddleglum helps Eustace and Jill find Prince Rilian and rescue him.
Bree and Hwin, Talking Horses (*HHB*)	Bree and Hwin carry Shasta and Aravis to freedom in Narnia.
Mr. and Mrs. Beaver (*LWW*)	The Beavers protect Peter, Susan, and Lucy from the White Witch and lead them to Aslan.
Deer, Centaurs, Unicorns, and birds (*LWW*)	These gentle creatures are sent by Aslan to rescue Edmund from the White Witch.

What do all these creatures mean for your life? They mean that even though you are not a grown-up yet, even if you sometimes feel small and unimportant, Jesus has big jobs for you. He will turn your ordinary life into something He thinks is extraordinary if you are willing to follow Him and do what He asks. You are never too small to talk to others about Jesus or too young to do things for others. You can walk a neighbor's dog, collect money for a family in need, or wash the car for your dad. You might even think of something to do that no one has ever done before. You were created to help change the world, and you don't have to wait to get started!

You are young, but do not let anyone treat you as if you were not impor-tant. Be an example to show the believers how they should live. Show them with your words, with the way you live, with your love, with your faith, and with your pure life. (1 Timothy 4:12)

Doctor Cornelius and Caspian's Nurse

→ *(Prince Caspian)*

His voice was grave and his eyes were merry so that, until you got to know him really well, it was hard to know when he was joking and when he was serious. His name was Doctor Cornelius.

Caspian's Nurse and Doctor Cornelius are two Old Narnians (Doctor Cornelius is half Dwarf) who remember what Narnia was like when everyone followed Aslan. Both of them play important roles in planting the seeds of faith in Caspian.

[Caspian] liked best the last hour of the day when the toys had all been put back in their cupboards and Nurse would tell him stories.

A mentor = someone older, wiser, and more experienced who wants to help you.

Their secret symbols of faith are that they represent the mentors you need in your life to help you grow in your faith. They are

96

older and wiser than Caspian, and they are able to take care of him, protect him, and teach him what is right and good.

JUSTIN TIME

In *Prince Caspian*, the trees eat different kinds of dirt at the Feast of Aslan. The menu is described as "rich brown loam" that looks like chocolate, pink-colored earth that is "lighter and sweeter," "chalky soil," and "delicate confections of the finest gravels."

Their faithfulness in their work is rewarded when King Caspian names Doctor Cornelius his Lord Chancellor (a high position in the kingdom) after Caspian takes over the throne, and Aslan heals the Nurse when she is dying.

DOCTOR CORNELIUS'S AND CASPIAN'S NURSE'S SECRETS

They are faithful in their work for Aslan, just like you should be faithful in your work for Jesus. Also, it is important to have older, wiser people who teach you things about Jesus, just like they taught Caspian.

Unlocking the Secret Symbols of Your Own Faith

Do you have adults in your life who teach you to believe in God? If so, who are they?

What kinds of things do you learn from these mentors?

Father Christmas

→ *(The Lion, the Witch and the Wardrobe)*

> *Some of the pictures of Father Christmas in our world make him look only funny and jolly. But now that the children actually stood looking at him they didn't find it quite like that. He was so big, and so glad, and so real, that they all became quite still.*

Father Christmas (you would probably call him Santa Claus) shows up in only one scene in *The Lion, the Witch and the Wardrobe*, but he is a very important secret symbol of faith. He arrives when Narnia has been under a spell for one hundred years of only winter but never Christmas.

Brrr.
Must be cold there!

JUSTIN TIME

C. S. Lewis said the Chronicles did not begin as books with a Christian message. "It all began with images; a faun carrying an umbrella, a queen on a sledge, a magnificent lion," he said. "At first there wasn't anything Christian about them; that element pushed itself in of its own accord." (from *Of Other Worlds: Essays and Stories*, C. S. Lewis)

The fact that it has been winter for so long means that people's hearts have turned away from Aslan, and Father Christmas is a sign that Aslan is about to break the Witch's spell. Father Christmas is a secret symbol of faith because Christmas is when Jesus, the Savior, was born on earth to save people from sin. Father Christmas symbolizes the coming of Aslan (Jesus) and the end of a terrible time.

FATHER CHRISTMAS'S SECRET

He represents the story of Jesus coming to earth to save people from their sins.

UNLOCKING THE SECRET SYMBOLS OF YOUR OWN FAITH

How did you feel when Father Christmas arrived and gave gifts to Peter, Susan, and Lucy?

What do you love about Christmas?

What kinds of things can you do this year to show that the holiday is more about Jesus than about presents?

Frank the Cabby and His Wife, Helen

➤ *(The Magician's Nephew and The Last Battle)*

 "My children," said Aslan, fixing his eyes on both of them, "you are to be the first King and Queen of Narnia." The Cabby opened his mouth in astonishment, and his wife turned very red.

Frank starts out in the Chronicles as a simple London cab driver (a cab back then was a buggy pulled by a horse). He ends up as the first King of Narnia after it is created by Aslan. His wife, Helen, who Frank calls Nellie, becomes the first Queen of Narnia.

Frank is accidentally pulled into Narnia just as Aslan is singing it into being. When stars appear and join in the song, Frank is so in awe that he says he would have been a better man if he had known something like this could happen. He is humble and a hard worker, and he knows instinctively how to show the proper honor to Aslan. When Aslan turns and looks at him for the first time, Frank automatically reaches up and takes off his hat as a sign of respect. This couple's secret symbol of faith is that they represent Adam and Eve, the first human beings Jesus created on earth. Frank and Helen are put in charge of taking care of Narnia and all the living things in it.

FRANK AND HELEN'S SECRET

This couple is an example of Jesus taking two people others would see as unimportant and using them to do something huge. If you seek after Jesus instead of seeking credit for yourself, Jesus can use you to do important things for Him.

He chose the weak things of the world to shame the strong. And he chose what the world thinks is not important. (1 Corinthians 1:27–28)

UNLOCKING THE SECRET SYMBOLS OF YOUR OWN FAITH

What good qualities do you think Aslan noticed about Frank to choose him as the first King of Narnia?

What good qualities are you developing in your life? Check out Galatians 5:22–23 to read some really good qualities we all should work on!

Secret Signs
in the Evil Characters

Not all of the characters in the stories of Narnia are "good guys," but even the wicked ones have secret symbols that can teach you about Jesus and the way He wants you to live. Mostly, the lessons you can learn from the evil characters are what *not* to do. You probably already know a lot of them, but it never hurts to take a look at what went wrong.

Here is a chart of the major evil characters in Narnia, what books you can find them in, what they did that was so bad, and how you can unlock their secrets that teach you lessons about faith. From the White Witch to the thoroughly bad Tisroc, these guys tried to destroy everything good that came their way.

Turn the page and turn
your head sideways
for the chart

NAME	WHERE EVIL APPEARS	WHAT EVIL DOES	SECRET SYMBOLS OF FAITH
Queen Jadis, the White Witch	*The Magician's Nephew*; *The Lion, the Witch and the Wardrobe*	Jadis represents Lucifer in the garden of Eden when he tried to give the fruit to Eve (Genesis 3:1–5). She tempts Digory to steal the fruit for his mom and to eat it himself. She also knows how to tempt Edmund where he is weakest (offering him his favorite candy and appealing to his desire to have power) just like Satan does to us.	Evil may look like it is in charge for a long time, but Jesus is still in control and He is coming back.

Uncle Andrew	*The Magician's Nephew*	Uncle Andrew plays with magic that he does not understand, like King Saul did in 1 Samuel 28 when he visited a fortune teller. It caused Saul's death and Uncle Andrew's eternal separation from Aslan.	When you close your ears and eyes to the truth for too long, you may never be able to see or hear it again.
Queen of Underland	*The Silver Chair*	It is tempting to give in to the desires your body has for things that are wrong, like Rilian does when he follows the beautiful Witch (in disguise).	Evil can dress itself up to look beautiful, but it is still evil.
The Tisroc	*The Horse and His Boy*	This Tisroc kills his own son and plots evil in secret, while trying to appear a good ruler on the surface.	Evil always gives itself away. It cannot keep up its disguise for very long.

NAME	WHERE EVIL APPEARS	WHAT EVIL DOES	SECRET SYMBOLS OF FAITH
Uncle Miraz	*Prince Caspian*	Miraz kills his own brother, the rightful king, and steals the throne from his nephew, Caspian. He is killed by one of his own lords, who wants the power for himself.	Stealing, whether it is a piece of candy or a kingdom, has serious consequences.
Tash	*The Last Battle*	The Calormen Rishda Tarkaan calls on his countrymen's "god," Tash, even though the Tarkaan does not believe that Tash really exists. When Tash really comes, the Rishda Tarkaan who called him becomes one of his victims.	Satan does have power. He is real, and he is not to be taken lightly. But he will be defeated in the end. Jesus is coming back.

There are other secrets about faith we can learn from the evil characters in Narnia. An important lesson is evil isn't easy to fight off, but it is important to confront evil head-on. It's probably gonna hurt if you do, because the devil does not want to let go of you easily. If the devil can get you distracted from following Jesus, then he keeps *Get lost, devil! You can't have me!* you from being able to shine your light to the world. So you have to fight hard to keep sin out of your life.

When Peter fought Maugrim the Wolf in *The Lion, the Witch and the Wardrobe*, C. S. Lewis wrote it as a bloody, kind of gross scene. This is not the only battle in the Chronicles, but it is the only one described in gory detail. Why? Because you have to fight hard to get evil away from you, but when you do, the rewards are great.

JUSTIN TIME

C. S. Lewis died in 1963 and is buried in the churchyard of Holy Trinity Church, Headington Quarry, Oxford, England, where he used to worship. It was built in 1849 and still holds services today.

EVIL'S SECRET

One thing to notice about the evil characters in the Chronicles is that they are always completely evil, all the way through, and they never change. Other characters in the books do some good things and some bad things, but they usually learn from the bad things and are sorry they did them. They are like people in real life, trying to get it right. Evil, however, doesn't ever try to be different. It is very clearly always evil.

Jadis never wants to go back to believing in Aslan, the Tisroc is not sorry for plotting against his own son, and Uncle Andrew never understands where he went wrong. Maybe C. S. Lewis made the bad guys this way on purpose so that when you run across evil things in your own life, you will be able to see them clearly and stay away!

Unlocking the Secret Symbols of Your Own Faith

When was the last time you did something that got you in big trouble? What were your consequences?

Were you sorry that you did it?

What can you do differently the next time the devil tempts you to do something wrong?

Evil May Look Like It's Gonna Win, but It's a Major Loser (with a Capital "L")

Since you just looked at the evil characters who hurt Narnia and its people, that brings us to Narnia's Greatest Secret No. 4—and it's one that should give you a lot of hope. Here's the secret: evil sometimes looks like it is winning for a while, but in the end it always loses. Sometimes evil takes control of a situation for years, but not forever. It will come to an end. The trick is to hang on to your faith.

When C. S. Lewis created the world of Narnia, he showed in his books that the forces of evil sometimes have the power for a long, long time. The evil Queen Jadis seems to run the show in Narnia for a hundred years, for example, and the characters and creatures suffer tremendously under her evil reign. Why? Aslan is certainly powerful enough to kick her out and get rid of her forever without even a little "meow," let alone a roar. Yet he doesn't—and it seems that he even disappears from Narnia for long periods of time.

Doesn't Aslan care about Narnia all the time? Why does he let bad things happen? This is the same question that people ask all the time about Jesus, and it is the fourth Greatest Secret of Narnia. Evil may seem like it's winning for a time, but it will not be in charge forever. In Narnia and here on earth, evil is present. The White Witch wants to be the ruler of Narnia, while the devil wants to be the ruler of our world. And in both places, the bad guys get to seem like the boss for a while. But only as long as Aslan—and Jesus—allow it.

Why does Aslan allow evil at all? Well, during the times that evil has power, the characters and creatures in Narnia go through a lot of hard things. They have to find hope in something to keep going. Through the hard times, many characters put their faith in Aslan and become believers in him. When things are going great, they do not need Aslan to save them. When things go bad, they need a savior.

Jesus may allow the devil to control things on earth for the same reason. He wants every person to believe in Him and live with Him forever in heaven. The Bible says that when He comes back to earth, people will be out of time to decide if they believe in Him. Once He returns to get rid of evil for good, those who do not believe and accept Him will be separated from Jesus forever.

So the bottom line is that Jesus allows evil because He loves everybody, as weird as that sounds. He wants to give us plenty of chances to live our lives for Him.

The earth will become useless like old clothes. Its people will die like flies. But my salvation will continue forever. My goodness will never end. (Isaiah 51:6)

Unlocking the Secrets of Swords, Stones, and Other Objects

Well, mystery solvers, you have unlocked lots of doors now and discovered many of the secret symbols of faith found in the characters and creatures of Narnia. You have also discovered some of Narnia's Greatest Secrets about faith.

There are more secret symbols to be found in some of the special objects that show up in the Chronicles. They can also teach you more about Jesus. You hold another key to unlocking the secrets in these special objects. Are you ready? Let's turn the key.

The Wardrobe

➤ (*The Magician's Nephew* and *The Lion, the Witch and the Wardrobe*)

And shortly after that they looked into a room that was quite empty except for one big wardrobe; the sort that has a looking-glass in the door.

The wardrobe from *The Lion, the Witch and the Wardrobe* is the first connection between the Pevensie children in England and the world of Narnia. It is the door that they travel through to get there. The secret symbol of faith that the wardrobe holds is one you can find in the very last pages of *The Magician's Nephew.* The author tells what happens to the core from the healing apple that Digory brought home from Narnia. The apple core was thrown out the window and grew into a beautiful apple tree. When Digory grew up and a storm blew the big tree down many years later, Digory had some of the wood made into the wardrobe.

The secret symbol of faith in the wardrobe is that even the objects of Narnia remember their creator and long to be where he is. The Narnian tree that Digory's apple came from was the Tree of Protection, which was planted from the life-giving silver apple that Digory brought back from the garden of the west where Narnia was created. That garden represents the Bible's garden of Eden.

Inside itself, in the very sap of it, the tree (so to speak) never forgot that other tree in Narnia to which it belonged.

That means that the wardrobe was made from a tree that was the "grandchild" of the special life-giving tree in the garden, and because its family tree (get it?) was so special, it never forgot where it came from. That's a great reminder to never forget your Creator—no matter how old you get or how far away you move from the place where you were born.

 ## THE WARDROBE'S SECRET

The wardrobe never forgets its creator, no matter how old it gets or how far away it goes.

UNLOCKING THE SECRET SYMBOLS
OF YOUR OWN FAITH

What steps will you take to make sure that when you grow up you never forget your faith in Jesus?

Think of three specific ways you can grow roots of faith to stay connected to your Creator.

The Lamp-Post

➤ (*The Magician's Nephew* and *The Lion, the Witch and the Wardrobe*)

She began to walk forward . . . toward the other light. In about ten minutes she reached it and found it was a lamp-post.

When Lucy enters Narnia through the wardrobe in *The Lion, the Witch and the Wardrobe*, the first thing she sees is a light ahead of her. It is the glow of a lamp-post, and Lucy wonders why there is a lamp-post in the middle of a wood.

That's the key to the secret symbol of faith in the lamp-post: it is a light that always burns in the darkness, just like the Bible says that Jesus is the light of the world, and just like He tells us to be lights to the world.

I have come as light into the world. I came so that whoever believes in me would not stay in darkness. (John 12:46)

Jesus tells people who follow Him to reflect His light to the rest of the world. You were created by a powerful God, and if you believe in His Son, Jesus, and have accepted Him into your life, then you have His light shining through you.

You are the light that gives light to the world. . . . You should be a light for other people. Live so that they will see the good things you do. Live so that they will praise your Father in heaven. (Matthew 5:14, 16)

The lamp-post reflected the light of its creator. Do you remember how the lamp-post came to be in the wood in the first place? In *The Magician's Nephew*, Digory, Polly, Jadis the Witch, Uncle Andrew, Frank the Cabby, and Strawberry the Horse all magically land in a world of "nothingness" after Digory touches the magic ring. The Witch still has in her hand the bar of a London lamp-post that she broke off and was hitting people with.

When the group hears Aslan singing and sees Narnia being created and coming to life, the Witch hates every minute of it.

 Ever since the song began she had felt that this whole world was filled with a Magic different from hers and stronger. She hated it.

In her anger, the Witch throws the bar from the old lamp-post straight into Aslan's face. It hits him

OUCh, DOUBLE OUCH!

and bounces right off. It doesn't even bother him at all. The bar lands on the new Narnian ground, and a few minutes later, it has grown into a brand-new lamp-post. Because Narnia was still being created, the ground almost instantly grew new life from anything that was planted in it. That's how the lamp-post came to be, and because it has the magic of its creator in it, it never goes out. If you have the spirit of your Creator, Jesus, in you, your light will shine forever too.

THE LAMP-POST'S SECRET

With Jesus in your heart, you can bring the light of God's love into dark places, like the lamp-post did in the woods of Narnia.

UNLOCKING THE SECRET SYMBOLS OF YOUR OWN FAITH

What do you think it means to be a light to people around you?

Tell somebody four ways you will let your light shine to others.

Turkish Delight

→ *(The Lion, the Witch and the Wardrobe)*

Each piece was sweet and light to the very center.

Turkish Delight is the name of Edmund's favorite candy, which the White Witch, Jadis, gives him in *The Lion, the Witch and the Wardrobe* in order to win him over to her side. It is a jelly candy, and Edmund likes it better than anything in the whole world.

JUSTIN TIME

Here's a recipe for Turkish Delight:

Take two cups of sugar and two tablespoons of cornstarch and dissolve in one cup of water. Add one-half teaspoon of cream of tartar and one tablespoon of rosewater. Boil to 220 degrees F. Cover the pot for five minutes, then pour into well-oiled shallow pan. When cool, cut into squares and roll in sifted powdered sugar.

(Hint: be sure to ask your mom or dad to help you make this!)

Turkish Delight in this story contains more than one secret symbol of faith. First, it is a symbol that the Witch, who uses evil magic, knows right where Edmund's weak spot is. She knows how to tempt him with his favorite thing so that it will be very hard to resist. There is nothing sinful in the candy itself, but the Witch uses it to tempt Edmund to make a bad choice. Does that make sense? Understand this very clearly—if sin was obviously awful and bad and no fun, no one, including you, would be tempted to sin.

Sin can be very attractive and fun—for a while. The second secret symbol is this: pretty soon, sin, like too much candy, starts to make you sick, like Edmund's stomach hurts after eating so much. After a while, Turkish Delight doesn't taste so good. After you get sucked into sin so deeply that it becomes a bad habit, it starts to have consequences and isn't nearly as fun anymore.

The thing to remember about temptation is that you always have a choice.

The thing to remember about temptation is that you *always* have a choice. You never have to do the sin, no matter how tempted you are. The best way to keep yourself from sinning when you are tempted is to run from that temptation. If you are tempted to get on the Internet and go to a Web site you shouldn't, get off the computer! If you are tempted to take something that belongs to your brother when he is not around, walk away from it.

The point is to move away from the temptation. Call friends over to help you, tell your parents you need help in this area—do anything and everything you can to keep yourself away from where Satan can get to you. Edmund could have chosen to not take the candy that the Witch offered. No matter how hard he might have tried to convince himself otherwise, in his heart Edmund knew the Witch was bad. As he looked at her, he saw that her face was hard and cold. He also didn't like the way the Queen looked at him, so he *knew* right from the start that she was not good. Still, he took what she gave him, and it cost him dearly. It isn't easy when something looks as good as Turkish Delight, but you *can* walk away from sin. The moment you are tempted, ask Jesus to show you a way out. He will.

Stand against the devil, and the devil will run away from you. (James 4:7)

Turkish Delight's Secret

The devil knows right where your weaknesses are, and that is where he will tempt you to sin. Also, although it may be fun to sin at first, pretty soon it's not fun anymore—and by then you might be stuck in it. The next time you are tempted to sin, run the other way!

Unlocking the Secret Symbols of Your Own Faith

Have you ever eaten so much of something that it made you feel sick? What was it? Do you still like to eat that food or candy?

Name an area in your life that might be a weak spot where you could be tempted. Now pray that Jesus will help you resist sin when Satan tempts you.

Father Christmas's Gifts
Sword and Shield, Bow and Arrows and Ivory Horn, Fireflower Cordial

➤ *(The Lion, the Witch and the Wardrobe)*

"These are your presents," was the answer, "and they are tools not toys. The time to use them is perhaps near at hand. Bear them well."

Although you already uncovered the secret symbols of faith in Father Christmas, now it's time to take a look at the secrets in the presents he brings to Peter, Susan, and Lucy. These three special gifts come in very handy and seem to perfectly fit each Pevensie who receives them.

→ unlike the shirt I got for Christmas last year

Some people think Father Christmas represents the Holy Spirit, the third member of the Trinity. In the Bible, the Holy Spirit is described as living in people who have accepted Jesus into their hearts. He helps you lead a Christian life by being your counselor, helper, and comforter. He helps you understand what Jesus created you to do by giving you spiritual gifts. These gifts are not presents for you like an MP3 player or a video game system. They are our special jobs within the family of believers that we are made to do, and the Holy Spirit will help us do them. Jesus says the Holy Spirit will help you remember what Jesus wants you to do.

But the Helper will teach you everything. He will cause you to remember all the things I told you. This Helper is the Holy Spirit whom the Father will send in my name. (John 14:26)

JUSTIN TIME

Mrs. Beaver has many of the qualities of the godly woman described in Proverbs 31. She takes care of her family and friends, even hurrying around her kitchen trying to get food packed for them when they need to start running for their lives. When Father Christmas hands out gifts to the Pevensies, he tells Mrs. Beaver he has left a sewing machine at her home for her. He knows that will make her sewing easier as she serves her family.

Father Christmas brings gifts to the Pevensies that they can use to serve Aslan and the other Narnians. Peter's gift is the sword and shield; Susan's gift is the bow and arrows and the ivory horn; and Lucy's gift is the diamond bottle of fireflower cordial that had healing powers. The secret symbols of faith in Father Christmas's gifts are what they represent in real life.

For Peter, the armor he receives seems a lot like the "armor of God" that Christians are told to put on in Ephesians 6:11.

Wear God's armor so that you can fight against the devil's evil tricks. (Ephesians 6:11)

The shield in this case represents faith, as the Bible explains in Ephesians 6:14–17, and the sword is the sword of the Spirit. When Peter uses this armor in battles, it protects him from evil.

The secret symbol of faith in Susan's gift of the ivory horn could be prayer. When you blow the horn, it calls someone to come and help you. If you pray to Jesus when you need Him, He always answers

(even though the answer may seem to take awhile or may not be the answer you were expecting). Also, your prayers always go straight to Jesus. You can talk directly to Him, just like the arrows sent from Susan's bow always went straight to their target.

Lucy's gift is the bottle of healing cordial, which represents the spiritual gift of healing.

JUSTIN TIME
Cordial is a stimulating medicine or drink.

JOSHUA'S JOURNEY

Q: Why didn't Edmund receive a gift from Father Christmas?

A: Edmund was not with his siblings when Father Christmas handed out these gifts. He was still with the White Witch. Edmund was later forgiven by Aslan for his betrayal, but his sin still caused him to miss out on some good things.

Each person who follows Jesus has spiritual gifts, and you can find out what the different gifts are in several places in the New Testament. Here are just some of the spiritual gifts you can find in the Bible:

SPIRITUAL GIFTS		
1 Corinthians 12	Romans 12:6–8	Ephesians 4:11
Apostles	Teaching	Prophets
Prophecy	Ministry	Pastor-teachers
Teaching	Exhortation (encourager)	Apostles
Miracles	Giving	Evangelists
Healing	Mercy	
Wisdom	Prophecy	
Helping		

Spiritual gifts may seem a little confusing, but the important thing to remember is that as you grow, the Holy Spirit will lead you to discover gifts and develop them in your life to use in serving Jesus.

We all have different gifts. Each gift came because of the grace that God gave us. (Romans 12:6)

THE SECRET OF
FATHER CHRISTMAS'S GIFTS

Peter's shield and sword, Susan's horn and bow and arrows, and Lucy's cordial all represent spiritual gifts. You also have spiritual gifts that can bless others around you as you live for Jesus.

Unlocking the Secret Symbols of Your Own Faith

Ask your mom, dad, Sunday school teacher, or youth pastor to help you take a spiritual gifts "test." These are multiple-choice questions that can help you discover where you might be able to serve in the church. You are never too young for Jesus to use you!

Ask older Christians who know you really well what spiritual gifts they see in you.

Pray that the Holy Spirit will show you what your spiritual gifts are and give you lots of chances to use them.

The Magician's Book

➤ *(The Voyage of the Dawn Treader)*

 She went to the desk and laid her hand on the book; her fingers tingled when she touched it as if it were full of electricity.

The Voyage of the Dawn Treader is a really cool book because it has lots of separate stories in it from each of the stops the ship makes. At the island where Lucy and the others meet the Invisible People, later known as the Dufflepuds, Lucy sees Aslan. She also meets the magician Coriakin (who is a retired star) and reads this really awesome magical book.

The book represents the story of Lucy's life, because she can only go forward in the book, not back. The secret symbol of faith in the Magician's Book is that it also stands for Lucy needing to "fall" and be saved, for when she is tempted to use a spell to hear what her friends are saying about her, she gives in to the temptation. Aslan corrects her and tells Lucy she was wrong to use the spell. Then he forgives her.

 JUSTIN TIME

Even though people were using ballpoint pens by then, C. S. Lewis wrote all of The Chronicles of Narnia using the old-fashioned pens that had to be dipped in ink.

Lucy reads the "loveliest story" in the Magician's Book but then cannot remember it fully. The way she describes it lets you know that it was the story of Jesus and how He saves the world. It has a cup, a sword, a tree, and a hill. The cup is the cup of suffering that Jesus talked about in Matthew 26:39 (and can also mean the cup of juice or wine that we sip for Communion to stand for Jesus' blood that was shed); the sword is the sword that the Romans used to pierce Jesus' side to see if He was really dead. The tree is what the cross is often called, and the hill stands for the hill where the cross was. Lucy leaves the room changed because of the book.

Jesus died on a hill known as CALVARY

THE MAGICIAN'S BOOK'S SECRET

The Magician's Book reveals that all of us, even people who seem really good and kind like Lucy, still make mistakes and need to be forgiven.

UNLOCKING THE SECRET SYMBOLS OF YOUR OWN FAITH

If you could use magic to find out something that you really, really want to know, how tempted would you be to use it? What would you want to know?

What do you think Lucy learned from this experience?

The Stone Table

➤ (*The Lion, the Witch and the Wardrobe* and *The Last Battle*)

> *The Stone Table was broken into two pieces by a great crack that ran down it from end to end; and there was no Aslan.*

The Stone Table starts out in *The Lion, the Witch and the Wardrobe* as the saddest place in The Chronicles of Narnia, because it is the place where Aslan lets himself be killed by the White Witch. But it becomes the most exciting and the best place in Narnia when Aslan defeats death and the White Witch and comes back to life.

The secret symbols of the Stone Table are that it represents the cross that Jesus died on to save the world from sin, and it also represents the stone tablets God gave to Moses that He wrote the Ten Commandments on. It represents the laws of God that were given to Israel.

The scene in *The Lion, the Witch and the Wardrobe* where the Witch and her followers beat and tease Aslan before tying him down and murdering him is very much like what the Bible says happened to Jesus before He was crucified. You should read the New Testament Gospels yourself to find all the ways the deaths of Aslan and Jesus are alike, but here are just a few:

- Aslan knew that he had to die. Susan and Lucy saw that he was sad, but they did not know why.
- Jesus knew what was ahead for Him on the cross, and His closest disciples did not understand why He was sad. (Matthew 26:36–38)

- Aslan's mane was cut off before he was killed.
- Jesus' beard was pulled before He was crucified. (Isaiah 50:6)

- The creatures with the evil White Witch made fun of Aslan.
- The Roman soldiers made fun of Jesus. (Mark 15:19)

- Aslan was tied down to the Stone Table.
- Jesus was nailed to the cross. (John 19:18)

- The Stone Table cracked in two pieces when Aslan died on it.
- The curtain in the temple in Jerusalem ripped into two pieces when Jesus died on the cross. (Luke 28:45)

- Aslan came back to life.
- Jesus rose from the dead. (Matthew 28:5–6)

The Stone Table is the place where Narnia was freed from eternal winter, and the cross is the place where you were set free from all your sins. It's the most important place in the world.

THE STONE TABLE'S SECRET

The Stone Table represents the cross that Jesus was crucified on. It also becomes the location of the last battle of Narnia, and Eustace, Jill, and King Tirian are taken to Aslan's Country from there.

UNLOCKING THE SECRET SYMBOLS OF YOUR OWN FAITH

Take a few minutes and thank Jesus for what He did for you on the cross.

If you saw someone who was about to be killed, would you be willing to take his or her place?

Magic Does Not Belong to People; It Belongs to God

The Chronicles of Narnia are fantasy books, which means they are filled with supernatural things. After all, have you ever seen a horse fly, a beaver talk, or a tree dance? The Chronicles are filled with magic, and that can be a sticky word for people who follow Jesus. The Bible says God does not want people messing with magic, so should you feel funny that you like these stories so much?

Absolutely not. C. S. Lewis uses the word *magic* instead of *supernatural*, probably because it is easier to understand. And the things Jesus can do *are* magical. Miracles are magical; coming back to life is magical; making a whole world out of nothing is magical. Creating a giraffe or a platypus is really magical!

 Ever since the song began she [Jadis] had felt that this whole world was filled with a Magic different from hers and stronger. She hated it.

What you need to understand about magic, and it's the fifth of Narnia's Greatest Secrets, is that magic belongs to Jesus—*not* to the devil, the angels, people, or the creatures of Narnia. When any other being tries to use magic, in Narnia or real life, it *always* backfires and causes destruction. And in the end, any magic other than God's loses its power. Jadis realizes this in *The Magician's Nephew* when Aslan is singing to create Narnia.

In *The Lion, the Witch and the Wardrobe*, Jadis's magic again is not as strong as Aslan's. He breaks her spell of winter over Narnia, and in the end she dies. In *The Silver Chair*, the Queen of Underland's spell is broken, and she is destroyed. In *The Last Battle*, Rishda Tarkaan calls on the god Tash, and to his surprise, Tash really appears. The demon Tash scoops up Rishda Tarkaan and takes him away.

TASH IS REALLY A DEMON 😊

When people try to have the kind of power that is meant only for Jesus, it's like they want to take control of God. Eustace recognizes this in *The Silver Chair* when Jill suggests drawing things on the ground or chanting to try to get to Narnia. Eustace says all those things are "rot," and he doesn't think Aslan likes them.

> *It would look as if we thought we could make him do things. But really, we can only ask him.*

That's what Jesus wants from you, to ask Him for what you need instead of trying to try to get it your own way. Learn the lesson about magic from The Chronicles of Narnia, and let Jesus be the only "Magician" you put your faith in!

God raised Christ to the highest place. God made the name of Christ greater than every other name. (Philippians 2:9)

The Tree of Life and the Tree of Protection

➤ (*The Magician's Nephew* and *Prince Caspian*)

The Witch whom you have brought into this world will come back to Narnia again. . . . It is my wish to plant in Narnia a tree which she will not dare to approach, and that tree will protect Narnia from her for many years.

Only a few hours after Aslan creates Narnia in *The Magician's Nephew*, evil has already entered it through the character Queen Jadis of Charn. Aslan decides to plant a Tree of Protection in Narnia to keep the Witch from coming near it. He sends Digory on a trip far away to pick an apple from a special garden and bring it to him. Digory finds the garden, and the tree inside is the Tree of Life.

When Digory picks an apple, he notices that Jadis has already picked one and eaten it, and she tempts him to eat one too. The fruit smells delicious and is beautiful, and Jadis promises Digory it will keep him forever youthful. She also tells him it will heal his mother and says he is being selfish if he gives it to Aslan instead of taking it home to her. Digory blocks out the temptation and takes the apple from the Tree of Life to Aslan. It is thrown on the ground in the newly created Narnia, and by the next day it has grown into a beautiful tree with apples. It becomes the Tree of Protection.

The apple trees' secret symbol of faith is that they represent in some ways the tree in the garden of Eden that God called the Tree of Life and in some ways the Tree of the Knowledge of Good and Evil that God told

Adam and Eve not to eat from. In the Bible, Adam and Eve did not resist temptation. They disobeyed God and ate from the tree, and it caused them to have to leave the beautiful garden of Eden forever. In Narnia, Digory resists the temptation and helps right the wrong he caused by bringing Jadis into Narnia in the first place.

C. S. Lewis gives us a chance to see what happens when someone does the right thing, and how it changes their lives—and the lives of many others. When Digory obeys Aslan, the Tree of Protection is planted and keeps peace in Narnia for many, many years. Plus, Digory still receives a special apple from Aslan to take home to his mother, and it heals her.

THE SECRET OF THE TREES

When you resist temptation and obey Jesus, good things come your way—and you do not put others in danger.

UNLOCKING THE SECRET SYMBOLS OF YOUR OWN FAITH

Name a time when you were really tempted to do something you were not supposed to. What did you do? What happened because of your choice?

Was it brave or selfish of Digory to give the apple to Aslan and not his mom?

The Pool in the Desert

 (The Horse and His Boy)

Before them a little cataract of water poured into a broad pool.

In *The Horse and His Boy*, Shasta, Aravis, Bree, and Hwin have to travel a long way through a desert to get to Narnia. It is hot and exhausting, and the mountains they see ahead of them never seem to get any closer. Finally, after traveling to the point where they are close to the very end of their strength, they find a little oasis in a valley. It contains clear, cool, delicious water; and they drink until they are not thirsty anymore.

JUSTIN TIME

oasis (n). 1. a small green area, usually having a spring, in the desert.

2. a relief, shelter, refuge

The secret symbol of faith found in the valley and the clear water in the desert is that Jesus always provides for you, even when you think you can't go on any longer. When you are sure that things in your life are as bad as they have ever been—that they are hopeless—that is when Jesus can show

up dramatically to show you He is there. He
is the life-giving water that Shasta, Aravis,
and the Talking Horses find.

*Jesus always provides
for you, even when
you think you can't
go on any longer.*

When you think you are too weak to
be able to handle a problem, that's when
Jesus can give you extra strength. The horse
Hwin teaches the others this when she says that she feels
she can't go on but that somehow they will be able to do it because they
are no longer slaves but are free.

It's the same way for followers of Jesus. The Bible says that once you
have accepted Jesus, you are no longer like a slave trapped in sin.

We know that our old life died with Christ on the cross. This was so that
our sinful selves would have no power over us, and we would not be slaves
to sin. (Romans 6:6)

THE POOL IN THE DESERT'S SECRET

Jesus shows up and provides for you when everything
seems really hard, and He helps you get through it.

UNLOCKING THE SECRET SYMBOLS
OF YOUR OWN FAITH

What was one of the worst times or hardest times of your life since you have been a follower of Jesus?

Looking back on it now, how was Jesus there for you during that time?

Dragon Skin

➤ *(The Voyage of the Dawn Treader)*

 Sleeping on a dragon's hoard with greedy, dragonish thoughts in his heart, he had become a dragon himself.

The story of Eustace turning into a dragon in *The Voyage of the Dawn Treader* is one of the clearest pictures in the Chronicles of someone being changed from their old sinful life into a new one. There are many characters who realize they need Aslan to change them, but Eustace *really* needs Aslan if he wants to be turned back into a boy.

he's obnoxious too

Eustace turns into a dragon for several reasons. He is greedy, selfish, and mean. There is not much to like about him before he becomes a dragon. As soon as he becomes a dragon, a change starts to happen to Eustace on the inside. He realizes that he needs people and wants them to like him. He knows that he needs to change for that to happen. That's the secret symbol of the dragon skin—it is a picture of what happens when you realize for the first time what the sin in your life looks like. Let me put it this way: it ain't pretty, and sometimes it even burns other people who get in your way!

Eustace's dragon skin is also a symbol of what happens when you finally quit trying to make everything better all by yourself. You can't be perfect, and you won't ever be perfect, so there's no need to put pressure on yourself to try to be perfect. When you try to be good all by yourself or try to make up for the bad things you do by doing good deeds, it is like trying to pull off your dragon skin. There is just more sin underneath. Only Jesus can take all of your sin and peel it away, making you clean again. When He does, it changes you for good. When Jesus gives you new life, you can keep the change!

The important thing is being the new people God has made. (Galatians 6:15)

THE DRAGON SKIN'S SECRET

When Aslan pulls the dragon skin off of Eustace, it is a picture of what Jesus does when you give your life to Him. Your "ugliness" is washed away, and Jesus makes you a new person inside.

UNLOCKING THE SECRET SYMBOLS OF YOUR OWN FAITH

Have you ever felt so grouchy that it was like wearing a dragon skin? How did you get it off?

When you have a bad attitude, what can you do to remember to ask Jesus to peel off your dragon skin and make you clean?

The Albatross

 (The Voyage of the Dawn Treader)

> *It circled three times round the mast and then perched for an instant on the crest of the gilded dragon at the prow.*

On another of the adventures in *The Voyage of the Dawn Treader*, the ship sails into a big patch of darkness. There is an island in it called the Dark Island. It is an evil place where people hear their nightmares come to life. The ship gets stuck in it, and Lucy whispers a prayer to Aslan to save them. Not long after that, a big white bird called an albatross appears in the sky and flies in a circle around the ship, then lands for just a moment on the front of the boat. The albatross then flies away and seems to want the ship to follow it. When the *Dawn Treader* follows the bird, they get unstuck from the darkness and are able to sail out into the sea again.

JUSTIN TIME

Albatrosses are some of the largest flying birds and can weigh twenty-two pounds.

When the albatross appears, no one except Lucy hears its reassuring voice. It is the voice of Aslan. The secret symbol of faith in the albatross is that it represents Jesus showing up in another form to help the people who follow Him. In old times, men who sailed the sea believed that if you saw an albatross, it was a messenger from God. Its appearance was always a good thing and meant that good things were going to happen.

JUSTIN TIME

The world of Narnia is flat. The *Dawn Treader* could literally have sailed off the edge of the world.

Lucy's faith brings help to the passengers of the *Dawn Treader*. Jesus shows that He may not always look like what you expect, but He always saves those who call on Him. The author C. S. Lewis even hints right in the book that the albatross represents Jesus.

At first, it looked like a cross, then it looked like an aeroplane, then it looked like a kite, and at last with a whirring of its wings it was right overhead and was an albatross.

THE ALBATROSS'S SECRET

When you need Jesus desperately, you can call on Him, and He will show you a way out of your trouble. Listen carefully so you do not miss His voice, and be prepared for His help to look different than you expected.

UNLOCKING THE SECRET SYMBOLS
OF YOUR OWN FAITH

In what unexpected ways has Jesus shown up in your life?

Ask your mom, dad, grandparent, or an older Christian to tell you a time when Jesus showed up like an albatross to save them.

Lion Skin

(The Last Battle)

Come and try on your beautiful new lion-skin coat.

In *The Last Battle*, the bad ape Shift puts a lion skin on the donkey Puzzle so he can fool the creatures of Narnia into thinking that the donkey is Aslan. This is an important secret symbol of faith to unlock, because it is easy to be tempted to act fake in front of other people. C. S. Lewis shows in this story how terrible things turn out when you pretend to be something you are not.

JOSHUA'S JOURNEY

Q: In *The Last Battle*, C. S. Lewis calls Puzzle an ass. Isn't that a bad word?

A: No. Ass is another word for *donkey*, and it was the word most people used back when C. S. Lewis was writing these books. So calling Puzzle an "ass" is just saying what kind of animal he is, not saying a bad word.

When you act like someone other than yourself, when you try to be cool or pretend that you know more than you do, you are saying (in a way) that the way Jesus made you isn't good enough for you. Jesus makes everything absolutely wonderful, and that means you are absolutely wonderful too! He created you to be the unique person you are, and He doesn't want you to hide your personality, your talents, and your gifts under an old lion skin. Jesus also does not want you to pretend to be something in order to get other people to do what you want them to do. You cannot control people through a lie, or there will be serious consequences. In the end, people will see through your act, and there will also be punishment. It just isn't worth it!

> *God created you to be the unique person you are, and He doesn't want you to hide your personality, your talents, and your gifts under an old lion skin.*

JUSTIN TIME

The Carnegie Medal Award is considered the highest award in children's literature, and it is given to one outstanding children's book every year. *The Last Battle* won the Carnegie Medal in 1956.

Once Puzzle gets rid of the fake skin and is out from under the bad influence of Shift, he changes his life around. He becomes a follower of Aslan, and he sees for the first time how wonderfully he was made. Puzzle was not stupid, like Shift had convinced him he was, but he needed true friends and Aslan to show him what he was really created to be.

The Lion Skin's Secret

You are great just the way you are. You should not pretend to be something you aren't to make friends or to get your way. Anything you get when you are pretending is just a lie and won't last. Also, make sure your friends are people who will help you be your very best and people you can be yourself around.

Do not be fooled: "Bad friends will ruin good habits." (1 Corinthians 15:33)

Unlocking the Secret Symbols of Your Own Faith

What times have you felt like you were pretending in order to get someone to like you or to do what you wanted them to do?

Which of your friends make you feel special just the way you are, and which ones make you feel stupid or want you to do things that aren't quite right?

Pray and ask Jesus to help you choose good friendships.

The Door

→ *(The Last Battle)*

> *Only a few yards away, clear to be seen in the sunlight, there stood up a rough wooden door and, round it, the framework of the doorway; nothing else, no walls, no roof.*

In the last book of the Chronicles, *The Last Battle*, there is a door that plays a very important role. The Door is the place where Eustace, Jill, and King Tirian (as well as others) pass from the world of Narnia into Aslan's Country. After King *Aslan's Country = HEAVEN* Tirian arrives, the Door plays another important role. It becomes the Door that all the people and creatures of Narnia either pass through into Aslan's Country or are turned away from—forever.

The secret symbol of faith in the Door is that it represents death. That sounds scary, but the way C. S. Lewis writes *The Last Battle*, it is a great reminder that for Christians, death does not have to seem scary. If you believe in Jesus, death is the beginning of a new adventure. It is simply walking through the doorway from earth to heaven. It is hard, because passing through death doesn't sound like much fun, but life goes on forever once you pass through. When you get through it, the new place is so exciting and wonderful and filled with family and friends and people you have always wanted to meet that going through the Door seems like no big deal at all.

It will only take a second. We will be changed as quickly as an eye blinks. (1 Corinthians 15:52)

C. S. Lewis's description about what happens after death is so exciting that it is hard to remember that Jill, Eustace, and King Tirian die on the battlefield in Narnia or that Peter, Edmund, Lucy, Digory, and Polly die in a train crash in England. If you did not understand all of what you read in *The Last Battle,* or if you have not read it at all, it's a great book to talk about with your parents or Christian adults you know.

THE DOOR'S SECRET

The Door represents death, and death doesn't have to be scary for followers of Jesus. It is awful, however, for those who do not love Jesus, because they will be turned away from heaven forever.

The death of one that belongs to him is precious to the Lord. (Psalm 116:15)

Unlocking the Secret Symbols of Your Own Faith

Before you read *The Last Battle*, how did you picture death? What do you think about it now?

Who are people you know who need to become followers of Jesus? Pray that they will get to know Jesus.

Those Who Are Sorry for Their Mistakes Are Always Forgiven

A s you have seen before, all through The Chronicles of Narnia, characters make mistakes—sometimes foolish ones and sometimes downright mean ones—but they apologize and are sorry. That's one of the Greatest Secrets of Narnia, and it's one of the greatest things you can ever experience: being forgiven.

Time after time in the Chronicles, characters tell Aslan they are sorry for what they did, and every single time they are forgiven. To make it even better, Aslan keeps the experience private between himself and the sinner, and the sin or mistake is never mentioned again.

If Aslan is like Jesus (and he really is), then you can trust that your deepest fears, feelings, and, yes, sins are safe with Jesus. He will never turn around and hurt you with the mistakes you admit, tell other people what you did wrong, or throw it back in your face later. That's how it is with Jesus, and that's what Aslan shows throughout the Chronicles.

For example, when Edmund betrays everyone in *The Lion, the Witch and the Wardrobe*, and Aslan has to be killed by the White Witch to pay the price for Edmund's betrayal, he doesn't go to Edmund and say, "Man, I can't believe you did such a stupid thing." Aslan doesn't go to Lucy or Susan and gossip about what Edmund did wrong. He talks to Edmund (a conversation

Edmund never forgets), forgives him, and then gives him the opportunity to use his new faith to fight for the right thing. Aslan not only forgives Edmund on the spot, but then he makes him a trusted friend. Isn't that awesome?

The sixth Greatest Secret of Narnia is that when you tell Jesus how sorry you are for the things you have done wrong, He always, always, always, always forgives you. Then, the Bible says Jesus throws your sins far, far away.

He has taken our sins away from us as far as the east is from west. (Psalm 103:12)

Edmund is only one of the people Aslan forgives in the Chronicles. When Digory brings evil into the brand-new world, Aslan forgives him. When Jill causes Eustace to fall over the cliff, Aslan forgives her. And when Aslan forgives them, the characters are always better off. They are nicer, more grown-up, more respectable, and more responsible after they are sorry for what they have done wrong and Aslan forgives them. For example, after Digory is forgiven, *The Magician's Nephew* says he could then look the Lion right in the eyes and feel absolutely at peace. When you are forgiven, your heart feels clean and light. That's peace.

The peace that God gives is so great that we cannot understand it. (Philippians 4:7)

Unlocking the Secrets of Narnia, Aslan's Country, and Other Magical Places

Your journey in this book is nearing its end, and only a few secrets remain to be discovered and unlocked so that your faith in Jesus can grow. You have learned a lot more about Jesus and your life with Him by unlocking the secret symbols of faith in the characters and creatures C. S. Lewis created in The Chronicles of Narnia. You solved even more mysteries when you took a look at the swords, stones, and other objects found in the seven books. Now it is time to journey to a few of the different places in the Chronicles, to discover the secret symbols hidden in Narnia, in London, in the Professor's house, in some of the islands visited by the *Dawn Treader,* and in Aslan's Country.

In each of these places, characters discover more about themselves and their belief in Aslan. Come along on a quick ride through the places of Narnia and beyond . . .

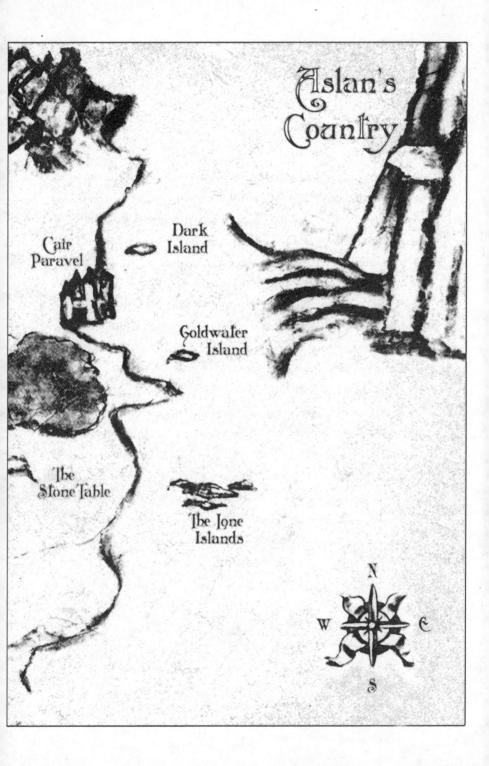

Narnia

Narnia is an imaginary world C. S. Lewis created in the Chronicles to teach you things you need to know about how to live a Christian life. It also shows you what Jesus did for you, but it is written as if it is all happening in another world—a fantasy, fairy tale–like world where cool creatures run around and kids go to magical places.

When a story represents something in real life, it is called an allegory. But C. S. Lewis said The Chronicles of Narnia are not an allegory. He said they are a "supposal." He said he was "supposing" that there was another world that was created, and you could "suppose" that Jesus came to it as a lion.

That's the secret symbol of faith in the world of Narnia, that everything that happens in Narnia is a picture of what it looks like for us to live in a world like ours—one that was created by a wonderful God, but one that also has evil in it. Narnia gives us a snapshot of what happened to our world when the Savior came and what will happen when Jesus returns and finally destroys it. Narnia has a creator and savior in Aslan, like our Savior and Creator is Jesus, and we can trust Jesus to the very end—which is really only the very beginning.

FOREVER IS A VERY LONG TIME

May the Lord bless you. He made heaven and earth. (Psalm 115:15)

London, England

London, England, is the home of Digory and Polly in *The Magician's Nephew*, and it is also the home of the Pevensie children before they are sent away to the Professor's house. London is the city where Uncle Andrew calls up magic and sends Digory and Polly to other worlds, and England is the place where the humans' lives end in *The Last Battle*.

JUSTIN TIME

London is the capital city of the country of England, which is on the continent of Europe.

The secret symbol of faith in London is the reminder that the same rules that apply to Narnia apply here on earth. In Narnia, the magic belongs to Aslan, not to the White Witch. In London, the magic belongs to Jesus, not Uncle Andrew. When you read about a character transforming from bad to good in Narnia, the change carries over to the character's life on earth as well. Eustace is a nice boy in London after Aslan removes his dragon skin he had on the island. Edmund is changed after he meets Aslan in Narnia and remains a believer when he returns home. Aslan tells the children that there are doorways to find him on earth too, and C. S. Lewis lets the reader know that getting to know the real Aslan—Jesus— is the reason the books exist.

There [in London] I have another name [Jesus]. You must learn to know me by that name. This was the very reason why you were brought to Narnia, that by knowing me here for a little, you may know me better there.

Once you meet the true Savior, Jesus Christ, your life is forever changed —no matter where you are.

The Professor's House

The Professor's house is a place of safety, a place of learning, and a place where the Pevensie children become believers in Aslan. It represents, in many ways, what the church is supposed to be today. Peter, Susan, Edmund, and Lucy are sent from London to the Professor's house to be safe from the war and the bombs that are being dropped on London. Once they get to the big country house, they go through the wardrobe and discover Narnia.

They also discover that the Professor is a wise man who makes them consider things they never would have believed. When Lucy says she has been to Narnia twice, Peter and Susan are worried enough about her that they go and talk to the Professor. He opens their eyes to the possibility that Lucy is telling the truth. The secret symbol of faith in the Professor's house is that it is the place where the Professor plants seeds of faith in the Pevensies' hearts and minds.

The Professor also presents a very famous argument for believing in Jesus that C. S. Lewis made in another of his famous books called *Mere Christianity*. In that book, Lewis says that Jesus must be one of three things: either He is not the Messiah but is pretending to be, making Him

Jesus— LIAR? CRAZYMAN? or Messiah!

a *liar*; or He is not the Messiah but honestly thinks He is, making Him a *crazy man*; or Jesus is actually telling the truth about who He is, making Him the *Messiah*. A lot of people do not want to believe that Jesus died to be their savior, but they will say He is a good man or was a wise teacher. But how can a man be wise or good, C. S. Lewis argues, if he is a liar or crazy man? The only choice left is to believe that Jesus must be who He says He is.

In *The Lion, the Witch and the Wardrobe*, the Professor tells Peter and Susan the same thing about Lucy: either she is lying (and she is usually very honest), she has gone crazy (and she certainly is not acting crazy), or she is telling the truth.

JUSTIN TIME

Truth is also another name for Jesus in the Bible, when Jesus says, "I am the way. And I am the truth and the life" (John 14:6). Jesus tells the people who believe in Him, "Then you will know the truth. And the truth will make you free" (John 8:32). In other words, if you know the truth, you know Jesus.

The Pevensies discover all of this through the wise teaching they receive at the Professor's house. You can discover a lot about Jesus from your pastor and teachers at church.

. . . .

Goldwater Island

Goldwater Island is discovered during *The Voyage of the Dawn Treader*, and at first it is very exciting. There is a pool of water, and at the bottom of

WOW!

it is a gold statue of a man. Wouldn't you like to discover a lot of gold just sitting somewhere, waiting for you to take it home? The problem with this place is the fact that the pool of water turns everything it touches into gold. So you can't get the gold man unless you reach into the water, and then you would be turned into gold yourself.

Goldwater Island's secret symbol of faith is that the devil likes to distract you by tempting you with a lot of things you want. Caspian was not looking for gold, but when he saw it, it tempted him. It is okay to want nice things, but sometimes Satan may tempt you to become greedy.

The best way to know what you should have and not have is to ask Jesus what He wants you to have. Is it really important to spend your birthday money on that new video game? Or would it be better to help another kid like you who needs the basic things like food and medicine? Believe me, it is hard to give up what you want. But once you see how good it feels to give, you won't even miss the stuff!

The Dark Island

The Dark Island visited by the *Dawn Treader* is an evil place that sucks in the ship and tortures its passengers by haunting them with their own dreams. The secret in this island is that it is like when the devil tries to get you to be upset about all the things you have messed up—even after you have asked Jesus to forgive you. Every time you hear the little voice

Don't Listen to the Devil!

inside telling you that you are not as good as the other kids, not as smart, not as talented, or that nobody likes you, you should imagine that you have entered the Dark Island.

Jesus wants you to have a life filled with good things to think about, do, see, and have. He does not want you to listen to lies. So the next time you feel down about yourself, do what Lucy did and ask Jesus for help!

- - - - - - - - -

Aslan's Country

Aslan's Country is one of the most fascinating descriptions in the Chronicles, because it is a very strong secret symbol of faith. It is obviously C. S. Lewis's imaginings of what the end of the world might be like, when those who follow Jesus go to heaven and those who did not believe in Him are sent away from Him forever. C. S. Lewis's description of Aslan's Country is so cool that it makes you really think about heaven as a real place. The Bible says that heaven will have streets of gold and gates of pearl. It also mentions mansions and thrones and feasts.

The 12 gates were 12 pearls. Each gate was made from a single pearl. The street of the city was made of pure gold. The gold was as clear as glass. (Revelation 21:21)

The Bible says those who live forever in heaven will have new bodies and will recognize each other. Beyond that, there isn't a lot of description of what heaven will look like.

C. S. Lewis's idea is that heaven might be a lot like earth—with familiar places and people—but much better. The food will taste better, the colors will be

Inquiring minds want to know!

brighter, and there will never be pain or hunger or evil. The characters in *The Last Battle* discover that the farther they go, the more "new" Narnias they discover, with each one better than the last.

JUSTIN TIME

According to C. S. Lewis, from the time Aslan created Narnia until the day he extinguished its sun and Old Narnia was destroyed is 2,555 Narnia years.

NARNIA'S GREATEST SECRET NO. 7

Death Is Not the End;
It's Only the Beginning

You've unlocked almost all the doors of the secret symbols of faith in the Chronicles, and hopefully you know a lot more about Narnia—and about Jesus. Now it's time to discover the last of Narnia's Greatest Secrets. (Well, the last one you'll find in this book. You can discover more as you read the Chronicles and your Bible on your own.) This is the most exciting secret of all, because you always save the best for last, right? Okay, here goes: the seventh of Narnia's Greatest Secrets is the truth that for the followers of Jesus, death is not the end—it's only the beginning! (You can yell and cheer here, unless your baby sister is taking a nap. If she is, cheer on the inside.)

Yep, it's true. In The Chronicles of Narnia, Aslan has a country far to the east past the edge of the world where all of his followers live forever. In real life, the Bible promises that Jesus has heaven, far beyond the edges of our world, waiting for His followers when they die. The really cool thing about the Narnia books, especially *The Voyage of the Dawn Treader* and *The Last Battle*, is the way C. S. Lewis describes what happens to people after they die in Narnia or in London.

Everyone wants to know what heaven is like, and no one who is living really knows yet. But C. S. Lewis helps you use your imagination to see how great it might be—how awesome it is to be reunited with everyone you love who has died before you. The characters show how exciting it is to discover a world where there is no sadness and pain and how fun it is to be in a place where you have all the time you want to explore, go on adventures, and never get tired of discovering something new just around the corner. For the characters from Narnia, Aslan's Country is a place where they can spend forever going "further up, further in" to discover even better Narnias as they go higher and higher.

When Aslan said you could never go back to Narnia, he meant the Narnia you were thinking of. But that was not the real Narnia. That had a beginning and an end. It was only a shadow or a copy of the real Narnia which has always been here and always will be here.

If you want to learn more about heaven and what the Bible says about the end of the world, the story is found in the book of Revelation. There are a lot of secret symbols of faith in Revelation, and many people have different ideas of what Jesus meant in some of the verses. But it is a fascinating book to read on your own, with a Bible study book to help you, or with an adult. Try making lists of all the main idea words, numbers, and symbols that are repeated in Revelation and see what you discover.

Before you study the Bible, pray that God will teach you new things about Him each time. When you unlock the secret symbols of faith in your own life, you will find a relationship with Jesus that—just like the characters of the Chronicles found—will last forever!

Jesus is the One who says that these things are true. Now he says, "Yes, I am coming soon." Amen. Come, Lord Jesus! (Revelation 22:20)

Unlocking the Secrets to Believing in Jesus

In each of the Narnia books, someone (sometimes lots of someones) is changed because of a relationship with Aslan. They are changed on the inside, like Edmund and Eustace, and they follow Aslan and become his friend forever. That's the whole point of the Chronicles, really, to paint a picture of what it might be like if the Jesus described in the Bible showed up in another world to save the creatures there.

If you felt something inside when you read The Chronicles of Narnia, or as you have unlocked the secret symbols of faith in this book, you are probably feeling the knock of Jesus on the secret door of your heart. The Bible says:

Here I am! I stand at the door and knock. If anyone hears my voice and opens the door, I will come in and eat with him. And he will eat with me. (Revelation 3:20)

What that means is that Jesus wants you to believe that He is real and that He did the things the Bible says He did. Like Aslan died in Edmund's place in *The Lion, the Witch and the Wardrobe,* Jesus was beaten and nailed to a wooden cross to die for all the things you have done wrong. He died in your place because He loves you, and so that you can live forever with Him in heaven someday. The Bible also says:

for God loved the world so much that he gave his only Son. God gave his Son so that whoever believes in him may not be lost, but have eternal life. (John 3:16)

Jesus wants you to get to know Him and invite Him into your life. You usually sit down and eat with friends and family, and Jesus invites you to eat with Him to show you that that's the kind of relationship He wants to have with you, as if He was your best friend or one of the family.

So how do you get that kind of relationship with Jesus? Well, after you believe that Jesus is real, you have to realize that you have done a lot of things wrong. The things you do wrong are called sins, and anyone who sins (and everyone has, even the most perfect-looking people) can't go to heaven and be with a perfect God. God is holy and good, and we are not.

All people have sinned and are not good enough for God's glory. (Romans 3:23)

Because we have done things that are wrong, there is a price that must be paid for those sins. Just like a thief who gets caught has to go to jail, people who sin must have consequences for their sins. The Bible says that the punishment for sin is death (Romans 6:23). But Jesus died to take that punishment away, if you tell Him that you are sorry for the things you have done wrong (and if you mean it!).

You may have heard someone call this the "Sinner's Prayer," and all it really means is that you need to tell Jesus that you are sorry for all your sins and that you are going to try—with His help—not to sin anymore. You can talk to Him out loud or in your thoughts, in church, in your bedroom, or with your parents. You can talk to Jesus anytime, anywhere, and He listens. You might not always feel or see Him (just like the children and creatures in Narnia never knew when they would actually see Aslan, but they knew he was always around). But you can have faith that Jesus is always there.

After you tell Jesus you are sorry, ask Him to be your best friend and to help you with everything you do. Thank Him for dying on the cross for you, and tell Him that someday you want to live in heaven with Him forever. After you have talked to Jesus, tell your parents or another adult you trust that you did it, so they can be excited with you. Now you are a Christian, and you can talk (pray) to Him anytime about anything.

To get to know Jesus better, get a Bible and start to read it. And find other Christians you can spend time with, so that you can learn more and "grow up" in your faith. Believing in Narnia is fun, but believing in Jesus is a lot better!

But some people did accept him. They believed in him. To them he gave the right to become children of God. (John 1:12)

THE SEVENTH KEY

Unlocking the Secrets of the Author, C. S. Lewis

When Clive Staples Lewis was born on November 29, 1898, telephones had only recently been invented and houses were just getting electricity. People didn't have cars, and iPods and the Internet were still one hundred years away!

Clive lived with his mother, Flora, his father, Albert, and his older brother, Warren (whose nickname was Warnie), in Belfast, a city in Northern Ireland. The Lewises had a big house with lots of small passages and overgrown gardens that Warnie and Clive, who wanted to be called Jack, played in together. Jack loved to read, and some say two of his favorite books were *Treasure Island* by Robert Louis Stevenson and *The Secret Garden* by Frances Hodgson Burnett.

When Jack was just nine years old, his life suddenly changed. His
mother got sick and died of cancer, and Jack and Warnie were shipped
off to boarding school in England. Jack hated the school and missed his
home in Ireland. The headmaster was very strict, and
Jack did not want to be there. Fortunately, in 1910 the
school closed, and Jack went back to Ireland for a year
before being sent again to England for school when he

The headmaster was declared INSANE!

became a teenager. This time he didn't hate it as much. Jack was very
smart and liked his studies. He had a private tutor who taught him a lot.
He loved poetry and was interested in foreign languages. He studied and
learned Italian, French, and German.

When he was eighteen, Jack got accepted at Oxford University. After he
started college, World War I broke out. Jack volunteered for the military
and became a soldier in the British Army during the war. Shortly before he
turned nineteen, Jack was shipped to the front line to fight near Arras,
France. He saw men die all around him, and it changed his life. In 1918,
when he was not even twenty years old, Jack was wounded by an exploding
shell and sent home to get well. The war ended just a few months later, and
he went back to school at Oxford.

Jack studied for four years in many subjects like Greek and Latin literature, ancient history, and English literature, and then he graduated
with honors. He decided to become a professor and began teaching
English at Magdalen College in Oxford. He taught there for the next
twenty-nine years.

One of the most important things that ever happened to Jack took
place in 1931, when he was in his early thirties—he became a Christian.
Because he wanted to tell the world about the faith he had discovered, he
started writing books. His first major book was called *The Pilgrim's Regress*,
which was about his journey to the Christian faith. He wrote many other
books for adults during his life, including a trilogy of science fiction

novels and other books such as *Mere Christianity* and *The Screwtape Letters*. Over the years, Jack became famous for his books.

A few years after World War II, when he decided to write children's books, Jack's publisher and even his friends tried to talk him out of it. They were afraid people wouldn't think of Jack as a serious writer anymore if he started writing for children, but Jack didn't listen to them. In 1950, *The Lion, the Witch and the Wardrobe* was published. Over the next six years, he wrote all seven of The Chronicles of Narnia. Believe it or not, many critics and book reviewers did not like the Narnia books, but ordinary readers did. As people started talking about them, the books became very popular and well loved.

During the time he was writing the Chronicles, Jack became pen pals with an American woman named Joy Gresham. Joy was a writer who called herself a "Jewish atheist" and a communist. Partly because she had read Jack's books about how he came to believe in Christ, Joy became a Christian too. They became friends and eventually fell in love. They married in 1956, when C. S. Lewis was fifty-seven years old. He became a stepfather to her two sons, Douglas and David. Sadly, in 1957, Joy was diagnosed with cancer and became very sick. She almost died, but the cancer went into remission for three years. Those were happy years for Jack and Joy. But Joy's cancer came back and she died in 1960, and Jack's health started to deteriorate after that. He died on November 22, 1963, the same day that President John F. Kennedy was assassinated in Dallas, Texas, and exactly one week before C. S. "Jack" Lewis would have turned sixty-five.

Since his death, C. S. Lewis has become known as one of the most famous Christian writers of all time. The Chronicles of Narnia books have sold more than one hundred million copies and are some of the most well-loved children's books in the world.

Doorways to
Other Adventures

The symbols of faith found throughout this book were uncovered by the author and her kids as they read and reread The Chronicles of Narnia. They also learned some things about Narnia by reading other books about this magical land. You can learn more about Narnia by reading the Chronicles, listening to them, visiting Web sites about them, and reading other good books.

Here are a few resources that can help you learn even more of Narnia's secrets:

. . . .

Books

Kurt Bruner and Jim Ware, *Finding God in the Land of Narnia* (Tyndale, 2005).

Finding God in the Land of Narnia is written by the same guys who wrote *Finding God in the Lord of the Rings.* This compact book offers short chapters that take a look at some key moments in Narnia—such as "Aslan's Song," "Evil Has Entered," and "The Sign of the Albatross" —and examines their spiritual meanings. Each chapter ends with a reflection to think more about.

Paul F. Ford, *Companion to Narnia: A Complete Guide to the Magical World of C. S. Lewis's The Chronicles of Narnia* (Harper SanFrancisco, 2005).

The encyclopedia-like *Companion to Narnia* has been around for more than twenty-five years, and it was updated in 2005. It has 530 pages of entries in alphabetical order on nearly every word in the seven books. It also contains maps, time lines, indexes, and many other tools.

Heather and David Kopp, *Roar: A Christian Family Guide to the Chronicles of Narnia* (Multnomah, 2005).

Roar: A Christian Family Guide to the Chronicles of Narnia is a 448-page book that goes chapter by chapter through all seven of the Chronicles. It has lots of color pictures, cool quizzes, fun trivia, and interesting facts about the Narnia stories. It is a book that is meant for families to read and share together as they explore the Chronicles.

Thomas Williams, *The Heart of the Chronicles of Narnia: Knowing God Here by Finding Him There* (W Publishing Group, 2005).

The Heart of the Chronicles of Narnia is a book for adults that goes deeper into the spiritual meanings and themes found in the Narnia books.

. . . .

Audiobooks

Focus on the Family Radio Theater, *The Chronicles of Narnia* (Tyndale, 2005).

This audio version of The Chronicles of Narnia is a nineteen-CD set that contains theatrical, unabridged productions of all seven books (or you can buy the books on CD individually). The productions were recorded in London and really take you into the action, with excellent sound effects. You can buy these at www.tyndale.com.

. . . .

Web Sites

The Chronicles of Narnia, www.books.narnia.com

The Chronicles of Narnia calls itself the official Web site for the C. S. Lewis novels, with descriptions of each book, sample chapters you can read (or listen to), a Narnia time line, games, and other features. This site was created by Walden Media, the same company that is making Narnia films in partnership with Disney.

The Lion's Call, www.thelionscall.com

The Lion's Call is a fan site dedicated to the Chronicles of Narnia. It contains writers' contests, book reviews, games, trivia, chat groups, a store, teacher's resources, articles, and facts about Narnia, and lots of art and illustrations of Narnia.

Acknowledgments

Thanks to Laura Minchew and Beverly Phillips, editors extraordinaire, for making this book a reality, and to copy editor Jennifer Stair for her insightful additions.

To Montine and Chad Pardue, for Chick-fil-A salads and free childcare (I couldn't have done it without you!). Thanks to Chick-fil-A (You're the best, John) and Starbucks in Spring Hill, Florida, for letting me take up booth and table space for days on end and not kicking me out even after closing.

I will forever be grateful for my wonderful husband, Adam, who always lets me go and do what I need to do and handles everything else without complaint. Finally, to my kids still at home—Lydia, Jessica, Joshua, Justin, and Amberlie Joy—you make every bit of hard work worth it.